GRAMMAR WORKBOOK

EXERCISES
in ENGLISH

LEVEL E

LOYOLAPRESS.

CHICAGO

Consultants
Therese Elizabeth Bauer
Martina Anne Erdlen
Anita Patrick Gallagher
Patricia Healey
Irene Kervick
Susan Platt

Linguistics Advisor
Timothy G. Collins
National-Louis University

Series Design: Loyola Press
Interior Art:
Jim Mitchell: 18, 24, 43, 68, 80, 86, 97, 103, 109, 120.
Greg Phillips: 16, 49, 51, 64, 112, 118, 123.
All interior illustrations not listed above are by Stacy Previn/munrocampagna.com.

ISBN-10: 0-8294-2337-0; ISBN-13: 978-0-8294-2337-2

Manufactured in the United States of America.

06 07 08 09 10 11 12 VonH 10 9 8 7 6 5 4 3 2 1

Contents

Name _Adriana_

1. Nouns

> A **noun** is a name word. A noun names a person, a place, or a thing.
> hiker   campground   tent

A. The following words are nouns. Write each in the proper column.

	PERSON	PLACE	THING
1. uncles	uncles	Los Angeles	keys
2. Los Angeles	Children	Walbrige Park	dashboard
3. keys	Williana	Cleveland	streetlight
4. dashboard			automobile
5. children			
6. Walbridge Park			
7. William			
8. streetlight			
9. Cleveland			
10. automobile			

B. Underline the nouns in each sentence. The number of nouns in each sentence is in parentheses.

1. <u>Mildred Taylor</u> wrote a <u>book</u> called _The Gold Cadillac._ (3)

2. The <u>father</u> in the <u>story</u> bought an expensive <u>car</u>. (3)

3. <u>His</u> wife had wanted to save <u>money</u> for a <u>house</u>. (3)

4. The <u>father</u> and the <u>children</u> drove to <u>Detroit</u> to visit <u>relatives</u>. (4)

5. The <u>mother</u> refused to go and decided to stay at <u>home</u>. (2)

C. Complete each sentence with nouns.

1. The next trip was to _Los Angeles_ and _N York_ .

2. They stopped at a _restaurant_ and a _ate_ .

3. The family spoke to a _interpreter_ and a _doctor_ .

4. They stayed at a _hotel_ and a _resort_ .

5. The children brought home a _picture_ and a _hat_ .

Nouns

2. Common Nouns and Proper Nouns

There are two main kinds of nouns: common nouns and proper nouns.
A **common noun** names any one member of a group of persons, places, or things.

    queen   **city**   **church**

A **proper noun** names a particular person, place, or thing.

    Queen Elizabeth   **London**   **Westminster Abbey**

A. Circle each common noun. Underline each proper noun.

1. Japan gave the United States some trees.

2. These trees were planted around the Tidal Basin
   in Washington, D.C.

3. Beautiful flowers bloom on these trees in April.

4. The blossoms are pink and white.

5. The flowers last for only 10 to 12 days.

6. Photographers from many countries take pictures
   of the blossoms.

7. The Jefferson Memorial is also decorated by
   these beautiful flowers.

8. In Japan the people have a festival when the first buds appear.

9. Washington, D.C., holds an annual Cherry Blossom Festival.

10. The United States received a beautiful gift from the people of Japan.

B. Complete each sentence with a proper noun to match the common noun in parentheses.

1. My Uncle Mike bought a new ___Lincoln___. **(car)**

2. Jessica shopped at ___Macis store___ for the gift. **(store)**

3. We went to ___Los Angeles___ for our vacation. **(place)**

4. After the game ___coach Fredy___ treated us to a hamburger. **(person)**

5. Carlos read ___The Giver___ for one hour. **(book)**

3. More Common Nouns and Proper Nouns

A. Write a common noun for each proper noun.

		COMMON NOUN			COMMON NOUN
1.	Canada	country	11.	Boston	state
2.	Brian	man	12.	Earth	planet
3.	Florida	state	13.	Sunday	day
4.	March	Month	14.	Alps	mountains
5.	Donald Duck	Character	15.	Pacific Ocean	ocean
6.	North America	Continent	16.	Abraham Lincoln	President
7.	Thanksgiving	holiday	17.	Memorial Day	holiday
8.	Beverly Cleary	person	18.	Thomas Edison	ivantor
9.	Brown University	place	19.	Buick	car
10.	Joe's Diner	restaurant	20.	Mississippi River	river

B. Write a proper noun suggested by each common noun.

		PROPER NOUN			PROPER NOUN
1.	man	Miguel	11.	mountains	Rainier
2.	country	Merico	12.	ocean	Atlantic Ocean
3.	singer	Madona	13.	statue	Liberty
4.	president	Obama	14.	general	Zapata
5.	astronaut	Jorge	15.	car	Toyota
6.	holiday	Thanksgiving	16.	inventor	Leonardo Da Vinci
7.	comic strip *Komica, Historieta*	Peanuts	17.	street	Iron St.
8.	lake	Patzcuaro	18.	store	Best Buy
9.	detective	Daniel	19.	movie star	Leonardo Decaprio
10.	game	football	20.	restaurant	Olive garden

C. Complete the sentences with proper nouns.

In ___July___ my family visited ___San Fransisco___ during the ___Independence___
    1. month   **2. place**   **3. holiday**

weekend. My friend ___Ema___ came with us. I saw ___parade___ for the
                 4. person   **5. thing**

first time.

Name _____

4. Singular Nouns and Plural Nouns

A **singular noun** tells about one person, place, or thing. A **plural noun** tells about more than one. The plural of most nouns is made by adding -*s* or -*es* to the singular form. For nouns ending in *y* after a consonant, change the *y* to *i* and add -*es*. For some nouns ending in *f* or *fe,* change the *f* or *fe* to *v* and add -*es*.

SINGULAR	PLURAL	SINGULAR	PLURAL	SINGULAR	PLURAL
nut	nuts	day	days	roof	roofs
bench	benches	berry	berries	wolf	wolves

Complete the letter by writing the correct plural forms of the nouns in parentheses.

Dear Mom and Dad,

I love visiting Uncle Ted and Aunt Maki

on their farm. One day we picked _peaches_
1. peach

and _cherries_. The fruit was so ripe that
2. cherry

we just shook the _branches_, and the fruit
3. branch

and _leaves_ fell off the _trees_. We had _bushels_! The
4. leaf   5. tree   6. bushel

fruit was then packed in _boxes_ and shipped to _factories_ where it
7. box   8. factory

will be made into jam. Soon the _jars_ will appear on our supermarket
9. jar

shelves!
10. shelf

Later in the week, Ted and I paddled _kayaks_ down the stream.
11. kayak

We saw two mother _foxes_ with their _babies_. I was really
12. fox   13. baby

surprised. I never expected to see wild _animals_ so close to the farm.
14. animal

I've been helping Aunt Maki a lot too. I get _vegetables_ for dinner right
15. vegetable

out of the garden. We have fresh _carrots_, _radishes_, and
16. carrot   17. radish

cucumbers every night. After dinner I help her do the _dishes_.
18. cucumber   19. dish

This trip has been my favorite of all my _vacations_!
20. vacation

Love,

Joey

5. More Singular Nouns and Plural Nouns

> For nouns ending in *o* after a vowel, form the plural by adding -*s* to the singular form. For some nouns ending in *o* after a consonant, add -*es* to the singular. Some singular nouns use a different word to show the plural. Some nouns use the same word for the singular and the plural.
>
> | SINGULAR | PLURAL | SINGULAR | PLURAL | SINGULAR | PLURAL |
> |----------|--------|----------|--------|----------|--------|
> | radio | radios | goose | geese | deer | deer |
> | tomato | tomatoes | man | men | salmon | salmon |
> | trio | trios | tooth | teeth | series | series |

A. Write the correct plural form for each noun.

1. child _children_
2. bison _bisons_
3. piano _pianos_
4. potato _potatoes_
5. mouse _mice_

   or maus

6. ox _oxen_
7. hero _heroes_
8. trout _trouts_
9. species _species_
10. moose _moose_

B. Complete each sentence with the plural form of the noun. Use a capital letter when necessary.

1. ranch   Cowhands work on _ranches_ in the American West.
2. burro   They ride horses and use mules and _burros_ as pack animals.
3. lasso   Cowhands use their _lassos_ to catch stray cattle.
4. wolf   They protect cattle from predators such as pumas and _wolves_.
5. calf   They brand _sheep_ with the ranch's brand.
6. sombrero Early cowhands wore _sombreros_.
7. sheep   Some ranchers raise _calves_ instead of cattle.
8. rodeo   Many cowhands compete in _rodeos_.
9. bronco   Men ride bulls and bucking _broncoes_.
10. woman   _Women_ compete in events such as barrel racing.

Nouns

6. Possessive Nouns

The **possessive form** of a noun expresses possession or ownership. The apostrophe (') is the sign of a possessive noun. To form the possessive of a singular noun, add -'s to the singular form.

architect   architect's

To form the possessive of a plural noun that ends in -s, add an apostrophe (') to the plural form.

farmers   farmers'

To form the possessive of a plural noun that does not end in -s, add -'s to the plural form.

children   children's

A. Rewrite the following, using singular possessive nouns.

1. the whistle of the referee   _____

2. the voice of the coach   _____

3. the horse of Paul Revere   _____

4. the badge of the officer   _____

5. the spurs of the cowboy   _____

B. Rewrite the following, using plural possessive nouns.

1. the cries of the babies   _____

2. the suggestions of both men   _____

3. the wishbones of the turkeys   _____

4. the carts of the golfers   _____

5. the tractors of the farmers   _____

C. Underline the correct possessive form of the noun in each sentence.

1. The circus (ringmaster's ringmasters') voice announced the next act.

2. A (lion's lions') roar caused excitement.

3. All of the (elephant's elephants') tails had pink bows on them.

4. All of the (child's children's) eyes followed the tightrope walker.

5. One (acrobat's acrobats') trick amazed everyone.

7. More Possessive Nouns

A noun has both a singular and a plural possessive form.

A. Write the singular possessive and the plural possessive of each noun.

	SINGULAR POSSESSIVE	PLURAL POSSESSIVE
1. doctor	_____	_____
2. baby	_____	_____
3. wolf	_____	_____
4. child	_____	_____
5. fox	_____	_____

B. Complete each sentence with the possessive form of the noun. Use a capital letter when necessary.

national parks 1. Grizzly bears are one of the _____ protected species.

Alaska 2. One of _____ claims to fame is the grizzly, a type of brown bear.

grizzlies 3. _____ bodies are massive, sometimes measuring eight feet long and weighing as much as 900 pounds.

cubs 4. A grizzly's den may contain cubs and the _____ food.

bear 5. This _____ claws are straight and not good for climbing.

camper 6. Every _____ fear is to encounter a grizzly.

food 7. _____ presence at a campsite can attract a bear.

human 8. A _____ response to seeing a grizzly can range from excitement to terror.

nature 9. Another of _____ wild creatures is the puma.

puma 10. The _____ many other names include catamount, panther, and mountain lion.

jungle 11. The puma is among the _____ inhabitants, but it is also found in mountains and deserts.

kittens 12. Its _____ behavior is very playful.

cat 13. A domestic _____ instincts are similar to a puma's.

deer 14. Many _____ lives have been cut short by hungry pumas.

hunters 15. _____ means of catching pumas are traps and open pits.

Nouns

8. Collective Nouns, Count and Noncount Nouns

A **collective noun** names a group of persons, places, or things that are considered as a unit.

   The <u>cast</u> and the <u>orchestra</u> bowed to the <u>audience</u>.

Count nouns name items that can be counted separately. Count nouns have singular and plural forms.

   The <u>students</u> and the <u>teachers</u> worked on the <u>projects</u>.

Noncount nouns name items that cannot be counted separately. They usually do not have plural forms, and they generally take singular verbs.

   <u>Lemonade</u> is made from <u>sugar</u>, <u>water</u>, and <u>juice</u>.

A. **Write a collective noun for each word.**

1. cows   _____
2. geese   _____
3. members   _____
4. actors   _____
5. musicians   _____

6. bees   _____
7. scouts   _____
8. singers   _____
9. bananas   _____
10. wolves   _____

B. **Circle each count noun. Underline each noncount noun.**

1. It's easy to turn raw vegetables into delicious soup.
2. Heat two tablespoons of oil in a large pot.
3. Chop one large onion and three stalks of celery and cook them in the hot oil.
4. Stir in one cup of sliced carrots and one large, chopped potato.
5. Add one small, sliced zucchini and one medium-sized can of diced tomatoes.
6. Slowly pour in six cups of stock or water.
7. Reduce the heat and cook for 15 to 20 minutes.
8. When the potatoes and carrots are tender, add one-half cup of pasta.
9. Stir in one box of frozen peas and one bunch of chopped parsley.
10. Taste the soup and add salt and pepper as needed.
11. Serve salad and some crusty bread for a perfect meal.
12. Shred one large head of lettuce and put it into a bowl.
13. Drain one can of artichokes and add them to the lettuce.
14. Sprinkle on some cheese.
15. Serve with oil and vinegar.

9. Nouns as Subjects

A sentence has a subject and a predicate. The **simple subject** is usually the noun that names the person, place, or thing the sentence is about.

The brave <u>firefighters</u> rushed into the burning building.

A. Underline the simple subject in each sentence.

1. Many tribes lived along the Atlantic coastline.

2. These Native Americans had lived there long before the arrival of Europeans.

3. Villages were located near lakes and rivers.

4. Six large tribes lived in the area from Canada to Florida.

5. Each tribe was an independent nation.

6. Some tribes had leaders called sachems.

7. A tribe's sachem could be a man or a woman.

8. A council of village leaders served with the chief.

9. The first colonists were helped by these Native Americans.

10. Chief Massasoit aided the Pilgrims.

B. Complete each sentence with a subject noun. Use each noun only once.

queen   island   **Arthur**   knights   sword
legend   king   wife   stone   court

1. King Arthur's _____ was named Excalibur.

2. A large _____ had the sword stuck into it.

3. _____ alone was able to pull the sword out of the stone.

4. The _____ of King Arthur was at Camelot.

5. Brave _____ such as Sir Lancelot attended the court.

6. The _____ of King Arthur was named Guinevere.

7. The _____ fell in love with Sir Lancelot.

8. One _____ tells about Arthur's sister, Morgan le Fay.

9. The _____ of Avalon was ruled by Morgan le Fay.

10. The _____ went to his sister's island to be healed of his wounds.

10. Nouns as Subject Complements

A **subject complement** is often a noun. It renames the subject and completes the meaning of a linking verb in a sentence.

SUBJECT   SUBJECT COMPLEMENT
Debbie is a fitness **instructor**.

A. Circle the simple subject in each sentence. Underline the subject complement.

1. Snoopy is a black-and-white beagle.

2. Charlie Brown is the owner of Snoopy.

3. Woodstock is a small yellow bird.

4. Woodstock is Snoopy's friend.

5. In the winter Woodstock is a hockey player on his frozen birdbath.

6. In the summer the birdbath is Woodstock's swimming pool.

7. Snoopy is a baseball player too.

8. Charlie Brown is the manager of the baseball team.

9. The other players are friends of Charlie Brown.

10. Charles Schulz was the creator of all these characters.

B. Complete each sentence with a noun used as a subject complement.

1. A famous school is _____.

2. In school my favorite subject is _____.

3. My teacher is _____.

4. The student across from me is _____.

5. In our school the principal is _____.

C. Complete each sentence with the correct subject complement.

    capital   **name**   **Dairy State**   **bird**   **range**

1. Wisconsin is the _____.

2. Denver is the _____ of Colorado.

3. The Sierra Nevada is a mountain _____.

4. Missouri is the _____ of both a state and a river.

5. The cardinal is the state _____ of seven states.

11. Nouns as Direct Objects

> The **direct object** answers the question *whom* or *what* after an action verb in a sentence.
>
> **After waiting in line for hours, we managed to purchase two tickets for the show.**
> (*Tickets* answers the question *what*—What did we manage to purchase?)
>
> **The show stars my favorite singer.**
> (*Singer* answers the question *whom*—Whom does the show star?)

A. Circle the direct object in each sentence. Write on the line whether it answers the question *whom* or *what*.

_____ 1. Connecticut claims two famous men from the American Revolution.

_____ 2. The state honors Nathan Hale as a hero.

_____ 3. At first Nathan Hale taught school.

_____ 4. Hale joined the army of George Washington.

_____ 5. Washington needed information about the British troops.

_____ 6. In his schoolmaster's clothes Hale crossed the British lines.

_____ 7. On the British side Hale drew maps of the British locations.

_____ 8. He hid the maps and information in his shoes.

_____ 9. Unfortunately, a British soldier recognized Hale.

_____10. The British hanged Nathan Hale for spying.

B. Complete each sentence with a direct object. Use each noun once.

battles	information	forts	town	marks
traitor	soldier	sides	hero	Benedict Arnold

1. Connecticut also produced a _____.

2. Americans remember _____ as a spy.

3. General Arnold first won _____ for the Americans.

4. Benedict Arnold changed _____ during the war, however.

5. This traitor leaked _____ to the British.

6. For the British, General Arnold captured two American _____.

7. During battle Arnold's troops killed every _____ in one fort.

8. His troops also burned the _____ of Griswald.

9. After the war Britain accepted its _____ as a citizen.

10. Nathan Hale and Benedict Arnold left their _____ on history.

Nouns

12. Direct Objects and Subject Complements

Read each sentence. Write DO on the line if the *italicized* word is a direct object. Write SC if it is a subject complement.

_____ 1. Tropical rain forests are the earth's oldest living *ecosystems*.

_____ 2. Rain forests cover only a small *part* of the earth's surface.

_____ 3. They are *home* to half the plant and animal species on the earth.

_____ 4. Torrential rains have washed most *nutrients* from the soil.

_____ 5. Rain forests have no dry or cold *seasons*.

_____ 6. A tropical rain forest has four *layers*.

_____ 7. The emergent layer is the tallest *layer* in a rain forest.

_____ 8. The canopy contains the most *food* for rain forest animals.

_____ 9. The emergent layer and the canopy receive the most *sunshine*.

_____ 10. Most rain forest animals are *inhabitants* of the top layers.

_____ 11. The fourth layer of a rain forest is the *understory*.

_____ 12. Tree roots, soil, and decaying material constitute the forest *floor*.

_____ 13. The understory and the forest floor receive very little *light*.

_____ 14. Large animals are *residents* of the forest floor.

_____ 15. Foods such as bananas, chocolate, and pepper are *products* of rain forests.

_____ 16. These foods are maintainable *resources*.

_____ 17. The Amazon rain forest covers an *area* about two thirds the size of the continental United States.

_____ 18. It is the world's largest *rain forest*.

_____ 19. Rain forests help control the world's *climate*.

_____ 20. Rain forests affect all *human beings* on earth.

13. Objects of Prepositions

Prepositions can show place, time, direction, and relationship. Some common prepositions are *in, into, on, to, by, for, from, at, of, with,* and *without.*
A **prepositional phrase** consists of a preposition and its object, a noun or a pronoun. The noun or the pronoun that follows the preposition is called the **object of the preposition.**

The group of <u>fans</u> cheered at the <u>appearance</u> of the <u>singer</u>.

A. Underline the prepositions in the sentences. Circle the object of each preposition. Some sentences have more than one prepositional phrase.

1. The bat hangs upside-down in its cave.

2. The sharp claws on its toes cling to the ceiling.

3. Bats sleep in this position.

4. At night the bat awakes.

5. Its lips push into the shape of a horn.

6. Squeaking sounds come from its throat.

7. The noise vibrates the air in the cave.

8. The bat listens for echoes from its squeaks.

9. From the echoes, the bat can "see" anything in the dark.

10. Bats are not blind in the daylight.

B. Complete the paragraph by adding objects of the prepositions. Add words if necessary.

My friends dared me, so I walked into (1.) _____. The insides were

covered with (2.)_____, but I kept walking. Soon I heard sounds

from (3.) _____. I felt a chill run down (4.) _____. I had

a lump in (5.) _____. My feet were stuck to (6.) _____.

Suddenly I felt a cold hand on (7.) _____. A cry finally came from

(8.) _____. Turning around, I saw a man with (9.) _____

in (10.) _____.

C. Write one or two sentences to finish the paragraph.

_____

_____

_____

14. Nouns as Indirect Objects

> The **indirect object** in a sentence tells *to whom, to what, for whom,* or *for what* the action was done. The indirect object comes between the verb and the direct object.
>
> | | VERB | INDIRECT OBJECT | DIRECT OBJECT |
> |---|---|---|---|
> | Sylvia | brought | Karen | souvenirs from her trip to Egypt. |

A. Circle the indirect object in each sentence. The direct object is *italicized*.

1. The Amendments to the Constitution give Americans certain *rights*.

2. The First Amendment guarantees people *freedom* of speech and religion.

3. The Fourth Amendment assures residents *security* against illegal searches.

4. The Sixth Amendment promises an accused person a speedy *trial*.

5. The Eighth Amendment gives citizens *protection* against cruel and unusual punishment.

6. The Thirteenth Amendment offered slaves their *freedom*.

7. The Fifteenth Amendment promised African American males the *vote*.

8. The Nineteenth Amendment gave women the *right* to vote.

9. The Twenty-second Amendment denies a leader a third *term* as president.

10. The Twenty-sixth Amendment assures 18-year-olds the *vote*.

B. Underline the direct object in each sentence. Circle the indirect object.

1. Mr. Rosenbaum assigned the class a project on the Constitution.

2. He offered the students any help they needed.

3. Maya read a small group the Bill of Rights.

4. Michael showed his partner a Web site about the Constitutional Convention.

5. Carl and Anna sent their senator a request for an interview.

6. Mr. Rosenbaum lent Laura a biography of Thomas Jefferson.

7. Tricia handed Mr. Rosenbaum her paper about John Adams.

8. Oscar told his classmates a story about Benjamin Franklin.

9. The principal promised the fifth grade a trip to Philadelphia.

10. The children sold their neighbors candy to pay for the trip.

Name _____

15. Nouns in Direct Address

A noun is used in direct address when it names the person spoken to.

Doctor, do you think I have pneumonia?

A. Underline the noun(s) in direct address in each sentence.

1. Folks, step right up and get your tickets.

2. Be careful, boys, going down the steps.

3. These are box seats, Dad!

4. Mr. Martinez, do you think we will be able to get autographs?

5. Maybe, Jim, we might get a few.

6. Fans, please stand for the national anthem.

7. Step up to the plate, batter.

8. I don't think that was a strike, Dad!

9. Jim and Todd, do you want hot dogs?

10. Do you want mustard, boys, on the hot dogs?

B. Complete each sentence with a noun in direct address.

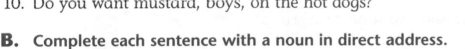

Mrs. Velez   Nurse Higgens   Coach   Rosa   Doctor

1. Where does your arm hurt, _____?

2. Bring me Rosa's chart, _____.

3. _____, is my arm broken?

4. _____, your daughter will need a cast for six weeks.

5. I won't be able to play in the game on Saturday, _____.

C. Write sentences, using each word as a noun in direct address.
Vary the position of the noun.

José   1. _____

Laura   2. _____

class   3. _____

Coach   4. _____

swimmers   5. _____

Nouns

16. Words Used as Nouns or as Verbs

A noun is a naming word. A verb expresses action or being.
Many words can be used either as nouns or as verbs.

VERB	NOUN

Be careful when you <u>step</u> on that crooked <u>step</u>.

A. **Write N if the *italicized* word is a noun. Write V if it is a verb.**

_____ 1. We often *visit* Philadelphia.

_____ 2. You should *plan* to go there.

_____ 3. A *visit* to Independence Hall is interesting.

_____ 4. Alexander Hamilton oversaw the *plan* for the Hall.

_____ 5. The delegates *debated* about the wording of the U.S. Constitution.

_____ 6. George Washington presided over the *debate*.

_____ 7. From Independence Hall it's just a short *walk* to the Liberty Bell.

_____ 8. Did the bell *crack* the first time it was rung?

_____ 9. The *crack* is about two feet long.

_____ 10. Next *walk* down the street to Betsy Ross's house.

B. **Write sentences, using each word first as a noun and then as a verb.**

1. design _____

_____

2. rule _____

_____

3. surprise _____

_____

4. judge _____

_____

5. ring _____

17. Words Used as Nouns or as Adjectives

> A noun is a naming word. An adjective describes a noun.
> Many words can be used either as nouns or as adjectives.
>
> ADJECTIVE   NOUN
> **The football coach tossed Jason the football.**

A. Write **N** if the *italicized* word is a noun. Write **A** if it is an adjective.

_____ 1. George Washington Carver was born a *slave* in 1864.

_____ 2. When he was a boy, *slave* traders kidnapped him and his mother.

_____ 3. He worked on a *farm* while he went to high school.

_____ 4. When he was 30, he went to *college* in Iowa.

_____ 5. Then he became a *college* professor.

_____ 6. He started studying the diseases of *farm* crops.

_____ 7. *Peanut* plants enrich the soil in which they are grown.

_____ 8. Carver is famous for inventing many uses for the *peanut*.

_____ 9. *Cotton* plantations were turned into peanut farms.

_____ 10. *Cotton* was no longer the main crop raised in the South.

B. Write sentences, using each term first as a noun and then as an adjective.

1. bicycle _____

_____

2. cell phone _____

_____

3. soccer _____

_____

4. truck _____

_____

5. pencil _____

_____

Nouns

18. Uses of Nouns

Nouns can be used in different ways.

S	subject	The <u>doctor</u> wrote the prescription.
SC	subject complement	She is a <u>surgeon</u>.
DO	direct object	She has a <u>degree</u> from Harvard University.
IO	indirect object	She gives her <u>patients</u> a lot of attention.
OP	object of a preposition	She practices with several <u>doctors</u>.
DA	direct address	<u>Doctor</u>, do I have a fever?

Underline each noun. Above each noun write its use. Use the letters given in the box above.

1. Shelly, did you vote in the election?

2. Yes, Erica, I cast my ballot.

3. Women didn't always have the right to vote in the United States.

4. They gained this right in 1920 through the Nineteenth Amendment.

5. Susan B. Anthony fought for this right.

6. She gave Congress her opinions.

7. She and a friend published a newspaper.

8. The name of their paper was *The Revolution.*

9. The paper gave readers a different view on issues of the day.

10. Susan B. Anthony also worked for a change in women's fashion.

11. She cut her hair short.

12. She even wore a type of pants.

13. Many people did not approve of this attire.

14. Women should thank Susan B. Anthony.

15. She was a tireless worker for the rights of all.

 Susan B. Anthony fought for women's causes. Give an example of how you can help a cause that you believe in.

Name _____

19. Reviewing Nouns

A. Write on the line whether the *italicized* noun is a count noun or a noncount noun.

_____ 1. French *citizens* gave the United States a gift in 1884.

_____ 2. This *gift* was the Statue of Liberty.

_____ 3. This monument was a sign of friendship and *liberty*.

_____ 4. Édouard de Laboulaye, a *historian*, suggested the idea.

_____ 5. The people of France donated *money* for the statue.

B. Write on the line whether the *italicized* noun is common or proper.

_____ 6. *Frédéric Auguste Bartholdi* designed the statue.

_____ 7. The statue was to be built as a proud *woman*.

_____ 8. Her *crown* was made with seven spikes.

_____ 9. The spikes represented the world's seven seas and *continents*.

_____ 10. She holds a book with the date of the *Declaration of Independence* on it.

C. Write on the line whether the *italicized* noun is the subject, the direct object, or the object of a preposition.

_____ 11. The *engineer* of the statue was Alexandre Gustave Eiffel.

_____ 12. Eiffel built the *skeleton* for the copper body.

_____ 13. Sheets of copper were hammered onto the *frame*.

_____ 14. Bartholdi's *mother* was the model for the face.

_____ 15. The two men shared their *talents* with the United States.

D. Circle the subject in each sentence.
Draw a line under the subject complement.

16. The statue is a female figure 151 feet tall.

17. The base of the statue is a pedestal 154 feet high.

18. The crown of the statue was once an observation deck.

19. The lights in the torch are powerful electric lamps.

20. The home for this great lady is New York Harbor.

Name _____

E. Circle the noun in direct address in each sentence.

21. Dad, do we really own that red convertible?

22. Yes, we sure do, Danielle.

23. Would you like to go for a ride, girls?

24. Do you want to come along, Grandma?

25. Sure. Molly, would you get my purse?

F. Write on the line whether the *italicized* noun is a direct object, an indirect object, or a subject complement.

_____ 26. Our last car was a *sedan*.

_____ 27. Dad bought the *convertible* from a nearby dealer.

_____ 28. It has leather *seats*.

_____ 29. The car is a beautiful *machine*.

_____ 30. Dad gave *Mom* a wonderful surprise.

Try It Yourself
Write four sentences about a place you know. Think about your use of nouns.
Check your spelling of proper, plural, and possessive nouns.

_____

_____

_____

_____

Check Your Own Work
Choose a selection from your writing portfolio, your journal,
a work in progress, an assignment from another class, or a letter.
Revise it, applying the skills you have reviewed. This checklist will help you.

✔ Have you capitalized all proper nouns?

✔ Have you used the correct plural forms?

✔ Have you used the apostrophe correctly?

✔ Have you chosen nouns that create a word picture?

20. Singular Pronouns and Plural Pronouns

A **pronoun** takes the place of a noun. A **personal pronoun** changes form depending on to whom or what it refers and to the role it plays in a sentence.

> The fishermen hauled in the net. Mrs. Murphy teaches school.
> <u>They</u> hauled in the net. <u>She</u> teaches school.

A personal pronoun is singular when it refers to one person, place, or thing.

> <u>He</u> is a computer whiz.

A personal pronoun is plural when it refers to more than one person, place, or thing.

> <u>We</u> were caught in a torrential downpour.

A. Write **S** on the line if the *italicized* pronoun in each sentence is singular or **P** if it is plural.

_____ 1. Our teacher read *us* a story about Harry S Truman.

_____ 2. *It* was from a biography by David R. Collins.

_____ 3. *I* saw the book in the library once.

_____ 4. Mrs. Raul read *it* to us a chapter at a time.

_____ 5. *She* always waited until after recess.

_____ 6. *We* could hardly wait to hear about Harry.

_____ 7. The Bowman twins like the part about *him* on the farm.

_____ 8. *They* lived on a farm too.

_____ 9. The Truman family owned cows; Harry milked *them*.

_____ 10. *He* had other chores to do also.

B. Write a pronoun to take the place of the *italicized* words.

1. *The Truman children* worked hard on the farm.

   _____ worked hard on the farm.

2. Early each morning *Harry* went to the barn.

   Early each morning _____ went to the barn.

3. He walked *the goats* to the public spring.

   He walked _____ to the public spring.

4. Mrs. Truman raised chickens in *a large hen house*.

   Mrs. Truman raised chickens in _____.

5. Every day *Vivian* gathered eggs from the hens.

   Every day _____ gathered eggs from the hens.

21. Personal Pronouns

A personal pronoun names the speaker; the person spoken to; or the person, place, or thing spoken about.

The personal pronouns that name the speaker are *I, me, mine, we, us,* and *ours.* (first person)

I wish the weather would change.   The book was a gift to **me**.
We wish Ming would stop by.   Sue and Harry waited for **us**.

The personal pronouns that name the person spoken to are *you* and *yours.* (second person)

Why don't you borrow my umbrella?

The personal pronouns that name the person, place, or thing spoken about are *he, she, it, him, her, his, hers, its, they, them,* and *theirs.* (third person)

He spent all the money.   Give the present to **him**.
She brought the fish to school.   Sarah would like to see **hers**.
They always make a lot of noise.   Does the officer believe **them**?

A. Underline the personal pronoun(s) that names the speaker.

1. Thoughtfully I waited on the stage for the spelling bee to begin.

2. We were all a bit nervous.

3. My teacher smiled encouragingly at me.

4. The judges gave us time to think.

5. As the words were given, I waited for mine.

B. Underline the personal pronoun(s) that names the person spoken to.

1. Have you ever been in that position?

2. You should try facing an audience!

3. Looking at them, you can feel everyone is pulling for you.

4. It is scary when yours is the first word announced.

5. Could you spell that word?

C. Underline the personal pronoun(s) that names the person or thing spoken about.

1. Joe was very nervous; he knew his would be the first word.

2. The crowd waited with him.

3. They all missed the same word that Joe missed.

4. Not one of them could spell the word.

5. Joe knew how to spell the next word, and he won the contest.

22. More Personal Pronouns

A pronoun can be in the first, second, or third person.
The third person singular pronoun can refer to a male, a female, or a thing.

> **He made lunch today.** (third person, male)
> **She set the table.** (third person, female)
> **It was beautiful.** (third person, thing)

A. Write **1** above the personal pronouns that are in the first person. Write **2** above the pronouns in the second person. Write **3** above the pronouns in the third person.

1. We want to give her a present.

2. She has been sick in the hospital.

3. Maybe we should give her a big helium balloon.

4. They will have some ideas for us at the gift store.

5. We asked him for some advice.

6. His was the responsibility for finding the right present.

7. When you saw it, we could tell you were disappointed.

8. It was a bunch of fake purple flowers.

9. I didn't like them at all.

10. We all thought they were gaudy.

11. You decided it was up to me to find something better.

12. But the present would still be from all of us.

13. I picked out a pink chenille robe.

14. My friends agreed hers should be pink.

15. We gave it to her with a nice card.

B. Write **M** above the personal pronouns that refer to males, **F** above the pronouns that refer to females, and **T** above the pronouns that refer to things.

1. She thanked and hugged him.

2. Then she tried it on.

3. He thought it looked good on her.

4. She was smiling when he left her that day.

5. He was happy that she liked it.

23. Pronouns as Subjects

Pronouns

> A pronoun may be used as the subject of a sentence.
> The subject pronouns are *I, you, he, she, it, we,* and *they.*
> **<u>They</u> laughed until tears were streaming down their faces.**

A. Circle the subject pronoun in each sentence.

1. I just read a book about Mathew Brady.
2. You must have heard of him.
3. He was born in Warren County, New York, in 1823.
4. At 16 he moved to New York City to study painting.
5. I was surprised at his young age.
6. Soon he started to learn photography.
7. It had just been introduced in the United States.
8. In 1849 he opened a studio in Washington, D.C.
9. He began taking photos of famous people.
10. They all liked his wonderful pictures.

B. Change the *italicized* word(s) in each sentence to a subject pronoun. Write the pronoun on the line. Use a capital letter if necessary.

_____ 1. *The Civil War* began in 1861.

_____ 2. *Brady and a group of photographers* took pictures of the battlefields.

_____ 3. *Brady* shocked the world by exhibiting the photos.

_____ 4. For the first time *ordinary people* saw the horror of war.

_____ 5. Later in his life *Brady* fell on hard times.

_____ 6. *Congress* bought his negatives for $25,000.

_____ 7. *My mother* is a big fan of Brady's pictures.

_____ 8. *My family and I* went to an exhibition of his photographs.

_____ 9. *These pictures* are the best known photographs of the Civil War.

_____ 10. *His work* gives us a visual sense of days gone by.

 Mathew Brady was always trying to improve his work. Give an example of how you could improve something in your life (a hobby, a project, a friendship, or some schoolwork).

Name _____

24. Pronouns as Subject Complements

> A pronoun can replace a noun used as a subject complement.
> A subject complement follows a linking verb and refers to the
> same person, place, or thing as the subject of the sentence.
>
> **The winner of the award was John.**
> **The winner of the award was <u>he</u>.**

**A. Circle the correct pronoun. Rewrite each sentence to show the subject
complement as the subject. The first one is done for you.**

1. The creators of the spectacle were ((they) them).
   They were the creators of the spectacle.

2. The actress who got sick was (her she).

   _____

3. The understudy who filled in was (she her).

   _____

4. The author of the scripts was (him he).

   _____

5. The orchestra members were (them they).

   _____

6. The observers of the events were (we us).

   _____

7. The talented costume designer was (he him).

   _____

8. The critics who panned the show were (them they).

   _____

9. The ushers for the show were (they them).

   _____

10. Was the ticket seller (she her)?

   _____

B. Complete each sentence with a subject pronoun. Vary your choices.

1. The confident film director was _____.
2. Is that cheerful makeup artist _____?
3. The most talented actors are _____.
4. The worried producer is _____.
5. The new camera operators are _____.

25. More Pronouns as Subject Complements

> A subject complement follows a linking verb and refers to the same person, place, or thing as the subject of a sentence. A subject pronoun can be used as a subject complement.

A. Underline the subject complement(s) in each sentence.
Write on the line a pronoun to take the place of the noun(s).

_____ 1. That boy is Brian.

_____ 2. The observer from the Boston Ballet Company is a recruiter.

_____ 3. The dancing teacher in the studio is Ms. Lane.

_____ 4. The advanced dancers are Brian, Ling, and Molly.

_____ 5. The piano player is Victor.

_____ 6. The man observing is Mr. Blanc, a retired dance teacher.

_____ 7. Is that Anthony warming up?

_____ 8. The best dancer is Molly.

_____ 9. The newest dancers are Marie and Caroline.

_____ 10. It was Marie who could do the most pirouettes.

B. Complete each sentence with the pronoun specified.

1. Was that _____? *(third, singular, female)*

2. No, it was _____. *(third, singular, male)*

3. The farmer was _____. *(third, singular, female)*

4. The best farmhands were _____. *(third, plural)*

5. The person on the tractor is _____. *(first, singular)*

6. Who is planting beans? It is _____. *(second, singular)*

7. The keepers of the chickens were _____. *(first, plural)*

8. Was it _____ who fed the pigs? *(second, singular)*

9. Yes, it was _____. *(first, singular)*

10. The farmhand in the overalls is _____. *(third, singular, male)*

26. Pronouns as Direct Objects

A pronoun may be used as the direct object of a verb.
The object pronouns are *me, you, him, her, it, us,* and *them.*

The president chose <u>them</u> to be cabinet members.

A. **Write on the line an object pronoun to take the place of the *italicized* word(s) in each sentence.**

_____ 1. At the Soapbox Derby I saw *motorless cars.*

_____ 2. Two friends built *a small wooden box with wheels and a fin.*

_____ 3. Katrina helped *Will* with the design.

_____ 4. Uncle Sharkey examined *the model* daily.

_____ 5. Aunt Dot encouraged *Will and Katrina.*

_____ 6. Finally the two friends finished *the project.*

_____ 7. At the race the officials registered *Will.*

_____ 8. The fin on the car puzzled *the judges.*

_____ 9. During the race the car with the fin held *the lead.*

_____ 10. Victoriously the soapbox crossed *the finish line.*

B. **Complete each sentence with an object pronoun.**

1. Will thanked _____ for helping with the design.

2. The audience applauded _____ as they received the grand trophy.

3. They held _____ high in the air.

4. The reporters wanted _____ to say a few words.

5. Uncle Sharkey treated _____ to lunch after the race.

C. **Underline the object pronoun in each sentence.**

1. Proudly Will carried it home.

2. The neighbors met them there.

3. Aunt Dot praised them for their work.

4. She wanted them to pose for pictures with the car.

5. A strong wind pushed it to fame.

27. Pronouns as Objects of Prepositions

> An object pronoun may be used as the object of a preposition.
> **The carefully wrapped present was for <u>her</u>.**

Circle the preposition in each sentence. Write on the line the object pronoun that can take the place of the *italicized* words.

_____ 1. Today the spotlight would be on *Joe Chapin and his classmates*.

_____ 2. The teacher looked approvingly at *Joe*.

_____ 3. For *Joe Chapin* class picture day was exciting!

_____ 4. The photographer gave directions to *the students*.

_____ 5. Then Mr. Ansel looked into *the lens*.

_____ 6. Next he glanced at *the flowering trees*.

_____ 7. The location near *the trees* was perfect!

_____ 8. The class moved across *the lawn*.

_____ 9. Again the photographer looked at *the boys and girls*.

_____ 10. Joe stood behind *the shortest girl*.

_____ 11. Mr. Ansel motioned toward *the last girl*.

_____ 12. Then he looked at *the sky*.

_____ 13. Rain fell from *some clouds*.

_____ 14. We crowded under *a shelter nearby*.

_____ 15. Mr. Ansel placed a plastic sheet over *his camera*.

28. Pronouns as Indirect Objects

> An object pronoun may be used as the **indirect object** of a sentence. The indirect object tells *to whom, for whom, to what,* or *for what* the action is done. The indirect object comes between the verb and the direct object.
>
> | VERB | INDIRECT OBJECT | DIRECT OBJECT |
> |---|---|---|
> | The baker <u>sold</u> | <u>her</u> | a <u>cake</u>. |

A. Circle the pronoun used as an indirect object. The direct object is *italicized*.

1. The children were bored, so Mrs. Edgars read them a *story*.

2. When she had finished, Carol gave her a *suggestion*.

3. Let's write them a *show*.

4. We can make them *costumes*.

5. They can sing us *songs*.

6. Please promise me some *help*.

7. Mrs. Edgars lent her a *song book*.

8. Billy was a good athlete, so she taught him some acrobatic *tricks*.

9. Maya was a good actress, so they assigned her a *role*.

10. If the neighbors want to come, we'll sell them *tickets*.

B. Rewrite each sentence. Use a pronoun as the indirect object.

1. The Good Witch showed Dorothy the Yellow Brick Road.

   _____

2. Dorothy brought the Tin Man the oil can.

   _____

3. The Wicked Witch denied the travelers any help.

   _____

4. The Wizard promised the Scarecrow a brain.

   _____

5. The Wizard showed his visitors a diploma.

   _____

6. The Tin Man asked the Wizard a question.

   _____

7. The Wizard granted the Tin Man a heart.

   _____

8. The Lion told the Wizard his wish.

   _____

9. Dorothy gave the Witch a splash of water.

   _____

10. The Good Witch gave Dorothy the directions home.

    _____

29. Subject and Object Pronouns—Part I

> *I* and *we* are subject pronouns.
> *Me* and *us* are object pronouns.

A. **Complete each sentence with the pronoun *I* or *me*.**

1. _____ raked the leaves into a pile.

2. Give _____ the rake.

3. That was _____ in the pile of leaves.

4. _____ put the leaves in garbage bags.

5. _____ have finished the yard work.

6. A little dog chased _____ across the yard.

7. _____ like the sight of colored leaves in the fall.

8. Dad will take _____ to the forest preserve to see the red and gold trees.

9. _____ will find pretty leaves and press them in a book.

10. Will you give _____ a paper bag for my collection of leaves?

B. **Complete each sentence with the pronoun *we* or *us*.**

1. _____ scattered popcorn for the birds.

2. Joe saved some for _____.

3. Did the squirrels see _____?

4. _____ must be sure they don't get the popcorn before the birds do.

5. What's the matter with _____?

6. It's not up to _____ who gets the food.

7. _____ should let whatever is hungry eat it.

8. Joe, will you give _____ some popcorn now?

9. It is _____ who should not have the popcorn.

10. Those two big bowls of it are too much for _____.

30. Subject and Object Pronouns—Part II

> *He, she,* and *they* are subject pronouns.
> *Him, her,* and *them* are object pronouns.

A. Circle the correct pronoun in parentheses.

1. (They Them) are the men and women working on the car.

2. A wrench hit (him he) on his hand.

3. Has (he him) found the problem?

4. (She Her) has given up trying.

5. All the parts puzzle (she her).

6. (She Her) prefers fixing bicycles.

7. (He Him) is a talented mechanic.

8. Mrs. Kervick will pay (them they) for their work.

9. Do you know (they them)?

10. (He Him) took his car to another shop.

B. Choose the correct pronoun to complete each sentence and write it on the line.

he, him	1. Is the youngest baby _____?
they, them	2. The baby followed _____ into the next room.
They, Them	3. _____ played with the baby until dinner.
she, her	4. The cook was _____.
He, Him	5. _____ put the food on the table.
He, Him	6. _____ is the boy nearest to the milk jug.
she, her	7. Nora wants _____ to eat the carrots.
They, Them	8. _____ planned to see a movie after dinner.
he, him	9. His little brother obeyed _____.
He, Him	10. _____ finished everything on his plate.
she, her	11. Erica told _____ about dessert.
they, them	12. Their mother asked _____ to do the dishes.
She, Her	13. _____ cleared the dishes from the table.
He, Him	14. _____ washed the dishes.
they, them	15. Their father drove _____ to the movie theater.

31. Subject and Object Pronouns—Part III

> The subject pronouns are *I, you, he, she, it, we,* and *they.*
> The object pronouns are *me, you, him, her, it, us,* and *them.*

A. Underline each personal pronoun. Write **S** on the line if the pronoun is the subject of a sentence or a subject complement. Write **O** on the line if it is a direct object or the object of a preposition. Use column 1 for the first pronoun in the sentence and column 2 for the second.

	COLUMN 1	COLUMN 2
1. He called her on the phone.	_____	_____
2. She told us.	_____	_____
3. We talked to him about the phone call.	_____	_____
4. The explanation from him didn't satisfy us.	_____	_____
5. Did he want her to come along?	_____	_____
6. Ask him to have lunch with me.	_____	_____
7. We talked about her over dinner.	_____	_____
8. He and I talked a lot.	_____	_____
9. According to him, she is the nicest girl.	_____	_____
10. And what does she think of him?	_____	_____

B. Circle the correct personal pronoun for each sentence.

1. (We Us) own four pets: a dog, a cat, and two mice.
2. The barking dog frightened (me he).
3. (Me I) heard the dog barking from two blocks away.
4. The one who really loves cats is (she her).
5. How sad that (you us) are allergic to cats.
6. (She Her) likes to play with the cat.
7. Ted put out food for (them they).
8. (Them They) scurry across the floor.
9. Have (you us) considered getting a pet?
10. Next week (we us) will feed the neighbor's rabbit.

32. Possessive Pronouns

> **Possessive pronouns** show possession or ownership. A possessive pronoun stands alone and often takes the place of a possessive noun. The possessive pronouns are *mine, ours, yours, his, hers, its,* and *theirs.*
>
> The blue skateboard is Cole's. His is the blue one.
> The green ones are TJ's and Joy's. Theirs are green.

A. Underline the possessive pronoun in each sentence.

1. Is that calculator yours?

2. Hers is on the desk in the second aisle.

3. Mine is in my backpack.

4. His is not here.

5. Do you think we lost ours?

6. Didn't the teacher say we could use hers?

7. I never lend mine to anyone.

8. Yours is older than Vince's.

9. I think hers is the most expensive.

10. Now I remember where ours is.

B. On the line write a possessive pronoun to replace the *italicized* word(s).

_____ 1. The leather-bound book is *Miguel's.*

_____ 2. I lost my book, but I found *Gwen's and Jessica's.*

_____ 3. My book was an early edition, but *Jeremy's* was a first edition.

_____ 4. *Julia's* is the lost one.

_____ 5. *Jane's and the teacher's* are the thickest and the heaviest.

_____ 6. Have you asked your teacher about *Jason's?*

_____ 7. *Ashley's* are on the floor in the closet.

_____ 8. My atlas is more current than *Vanessa's.*

_____ 9. Do you care if I highlight your book or *David's?*

_____ 10. *Tom's and Jessica's* are on that table in the corner.

33. Possessive Adjectives

A **possessive adjective** shows possession or ownership. A possessive adjective goes before a noun. The possessive adjectives are *my, your, his, her, its, our, your,* and *their.*

SINGULAR   **my necklace**   **your sandwich**   **his/her/its bowl**
PLURAL   **our footballs**   **your sweaters**   **their magazines**

A. Underline the possessive adjective(s) in each sentence.

1. Our class had its own competition.
2. Everyone kept his or her own score.
3. The events tested your silliness.
4. We paddled our skateboards with plungers.
5. I had trouble keeping my feet on the skateboard.
6. Walking a floor balance beam, Teresa kept the book on her head.
7. Ichiro made his prize-winning beard out of shaving cream.
8. Kate used aluminum foil to make her hat.
9. How high can you count with a pencil between your nose and top lip?
10. The boys were able to hold pencils behind their ears better than the girls were.

B. Write A if the underlined word is an adjective. Write P if it is a pronoun.

_____ 1. Their reasons for not winning were many.

_____ 2. The stick and its plunger did not stay together.

_____ 3. Didn't they use glue on theirs?

_____ 4. The stick that broke was his.

_____ 5. Your technique was certainly good!

_____ 6. Denny's ears are bigger than mine.

_____ 7. It's not my fault that they're bigger than yours.

_____ 8. Her skill at ear wiggling is unmatched.

_____ 9. I think the silliest stunt was ours.

_____ 10. This was certainly our most unusual day!

Pronouns

34. Intensive Pronouns, Reflexive Pronouns

Intensive and reflexive pronouns end in *-self* or *-selves*. An **intensive pronoun** emphasizes a noun that precedes it. A **reflexive pronoun** is used as a direct object or an indirect object of a verb or as the object of a preposition.

SINGULAR	myself	yourself	himself	herself	itself
PLURAL	ourselves	yourselves	themselves		

INTENSIVE   She herself made a costume. (emphasis)
REFLEXIVE   She made herself a costume. (indirect object)

A. Underline the reflexive or intensive pronoun in each sentence.
Write **I** on the line if it is intensive and **R** if it is reflexive.

_____ 1. At the school play I saw him myself.

_____ 2. Did you audition for the play yourself?

_____ 3. I myself have been backstage.

_____ 4. The student usher closed the doors himself.

_____ 5. The teacher herself arranged the stage lighting.

_____ 6. The empty stage itself looks very large and intimidating.

_____ 7. The girls amused themselves while waiting for the play to begin.

_____ 8. Prepare yourself for a spectacular performance.

_____ 9. Suddenly I found myself lost in the action of the play.

_____ 10. The hurt actor blamed nobody but himself for the accident.

B. Complete each sentence with a correct pronoun.
On the line write **R** for reflexive or **I** for intensive.

_____ 1. The boys _____ wanted to cut the birthday cake.

_____ 2. Tina _____ made the cake from scratch.

_____ 3. You can all help _____ to some ice cream.

_____ 4. They helped _____ to the cake.

_____ 5. The cake _____ was covered with pink frosting and flowers.

_____ 6. The guests exhausted _____ by singing for the birthday girl.

_____ 7. I laughed at _____ for being so giddy.

_____ 8. We _____ helped clean up after the party.

_____ 9. Mike the Magician _____ entertained the guests.

_____ 10. What present did you _____ bring, Katy?

35. Antecedents

> The word to which a pronoun refers is its **antecedent.** The pronoun must agree with its antecedent in number and in whether it refers to a male, a female, or a thing.
>
> ANTECEDENT   PRONOUN
> <u>Dolley Madison</u> was born in South Carolina, but <u>she</u> grew up in Pennsylvania.

A. Circle the pronoun for the *italicized* antecedent.

1. Dolley Payne married *John Todd, Jr.,* in 1790, but he died three years later.

2. The young *widow* was charming, and James Madison was attracted to her.

3. *James* and *Dolley* were of different religions, but they married in 1794.

4. *Dolley* was a Quaker, but she chose a fashionable dress for the wedding.

5. Dolley's *son* lived with the couple, and James was patient with him.

B. Circle the antecedent for the *italicized* pronoun.

1. James Madison was a member of Congress; in 1801 *he* became Secretary of State.

2. James moved into the White House with Dolley when the people elected *him* president.

3. Dolley assisted at the White House whenever James asked *her* to.

4. Diplomats came from all over the world, and Dolley welcomed *them.*

5. Dolley fled the White House when the British set *it* on fire.

C. Complete each sentence with a pronoun. The antecedent is *italicized*.

1. *James* wrote to Dolley that the enemy was greater than _____ thought.

2. He said that *troops* were coming and that she should escape from _____.

3. Dolley was determined to save official *papers,* so she stuffed _____ into trunks.

4. A *portrait* of George Washington was precious, but _____ was fastened to the wall with screws.

5. *Dolley* had the frame broken so that _____ could save the famous painting.

6. She gave the picture to two *gentlemen* and asked _____ to take it to New York.

7. *Dolley* and *James* met outside Washington, and _____ watched the city burn.

8. Years later Dolley moved with *James* to his plantation after _____ retired.

9. After James died, *Dolley* moved back to Washington, where friends helped _____.

10. By the time *Dolley* died in 1849, _____ was beloved by all.

36. Pronouns and Contractions

> A **contraction** is made by joining two words. A contraction has an apostrophe. The apostrophe replaces one or more letters. Personal pronouns can be joined with some verbs to form contractions.
>
> | I am | I'm | | we have | we've |
> |------|-----|--|---------|-------|
> | you are | you're | | he will | he'll |
> | she is | she's | | they will | they'll |

A. Change each set of words in parentheses to a contraction.
Write the contraction on the line. Use a capital letter when necessary.

1. (I am) _____ reading about Boys' Festival Day in Japan.

2. On that day (they will) _____ try to fly a 1,600-pound kite.

3. (It is) _____ an event everyone is looking forward to.

4. (They will) _____ paint a fish on the kite.

5. (I have) _____ learned that the fish is a symbol of courage.

6. (We are) _____ going to have a kite-flying day at our school.

7. Mrs. Kelly says (she is) _____ a great kite flyer.

8. (We will) _____ see how high her kite goes.

9. (You are) _____ going to fly your kite, aren't you?

10. (It will) _____ be a lot of fun.

B. Circle the correct word to complete each sentence.

1. The students are going to use (they're their) math, art, and science skills.

2. (They're Their) going to make kites.

3. Mrs. Kelly said that (you're your) kite looks beautiful.

4. I hope (you're your) not going to fly that work of art!

5. (It's Its) exciting to fly a kite.

6. You hold the kite up by (it's its) tail.

7. (Your You're) going to run as fast as you can.

8. The students took (they're their) kites outside.

9. (They're their) running across the field.

10. Don't let (it's its) string get caught in a tree!

37. Demonstrative Pronouns, Interrogative Pronouns

Pronouns

Demonstrative pronouns are used to point out people, places, or things.

	SINGULAR	PLURAL
NEAR	this	these
FAR	that	those

Interrogative pronouns are used to ask questions.
<u>Who</u> owns this bike?   <u>Whom</u> did you teach to ride?
<u>Whose</u> is this skateboard?   <u>What</u> is the best skate park in town?

A. Circle the demonstrative pronoun in each sentence.
Tell whether it is singular or plural.

_____ 1. This is my favorite recipe.

_____ 2. These are the ingredients we need.

_____ 3. I'll put the batter in this.

_____ 4. That is the spoon I'll use.

_____ 5. Please hand those to me.

B. Complete each sentence with a demonstrative pronoun.
Follow the directions in parentheses.

1. _____ is my old soccer uniform. *(singular, near)*

2. _____ are my old shoes. *(plural, far)*

3. I can't wear _____ now. *(plural, near)*

4. _____ has been in my closet for months. *(singular, far)*

5. I think I'll give _____ to charity. *(plural, near)*

C. Circle the correct interrogative pronoun to complete each sentence.

1. (Who Whom) was Martha Dandridge Custis?

2. (Who Whom) did she marry?

3. (What Whose) was her husband George Washington like?

4. (Who Whose) was the house they lived in?

5. (Who Whose) called her a wonderful character?

6. (Who Whose) was called away from his wife by battles?

7. (Whose What) was their home called?

8. (What Who) did Martha write in her letters?

9. To (who whom) did they say goodbye?

10. (Who Whom) burned George Washington's papers after he died?

Name _____

38. Reviewing Pronouns

A. On the line write **1** if the *italicized* pronoun is the speaker, **2** if it is the person spoken to, or **3** if it is the person spoken about.

_____ 1. Clara Barton said, "*We* need wagons for the medical supplies."

_____ 2. "*We* don't have horses for the wagons," the Secretary of War told her.

_____ 3. "*You* can't allow the men to be without these things," she said.

_____ 4. "*They* need medical supplies badly."

_____ 5. "*You* are a brave woman," he told her.

_____ 6. "Mr. Stanton, allow *me* to go to the battlefield," she replied.

_____ 7. "That is the place where *I* am needed most."

_____ 8. She added that the wounded required attention before *they* were moved.

_____ 9. "Nursing *them* on the battlefield is necessary," Miss Barton insisted.

_____ 10. "*You* could get hurt if fighting were to erupt," the Secretary replied.

B. Circle the reflexive or intensive pronoun in each sentence. Write **R** on the line if the pronoun is reflexive and **I** if it is intensive.

_____ 11. She herself was called the Angel of the Battlefield.

_____ 12. "Clara, prepare yourself for the worst," the officers warned.

_____ 13. The men helped themselves the best they could.

_____ 14. I myself could never do what Clara did.

_____ 15. The work itself was difficult, but Clara was determined.

C. On the line write **S** if the *italicized* pronoun is the subject.
Write **SC** if it is the subject complement.

_____ 16. Our swimming teacher is *she.*

_____ 17. *She* taught my brother Christopher.

_____ 18. The lifeguard is *he.*

_____ 19. At the pool *he* got his swimming badge.

_____ 20. *He* takes his responsibility seriously.

CONTINUED

D. Write the correct pronoun on the line.

I, me   21. One day Mrs. Perez asked _____ to read to the class.

She, Her   22. _____ handed me the book.

We, Us   23. _____ were reading Harry Truman's biography.

He, Him   24. _____ had many responsibilities as a child.

they, them   25. Harry did his best with each of _____.

E. Write on the line a possessive pronoun for the *italicized* words in each sentence.

_____ 26. My family's home is in Missouri, near *Harry Truman's.*

_____ 27. My great grandparents' farm was next to *the Trumans'.*

_____ 28. Unlike *most people's,* Mr. Truman's middle name was a letter.

_____ 29. In my report about historic homes, *James Madison's* came first.

_____ 30. *Barbara Jordan's* may become a tourist destination.

F. Write the contraction on the line.

31. we will   _____   34. he is   _____

32. you have   _____   35. they are   _____

33. it will   _____

Try It Yourself

**Write four sentences about a memorable character you have
known or read about. Be sure you use pronouns correctly.**

_____

_____

_____

_____

Check Your Own Work

**Choose a selection from your writing portfolio, your journal, a work in progress,
an assignment from another class, or a letter. Revise it, applying the skills you have
reviewed. This checklist below will help you.**

✔ Do your pronouns reflect the correct number and person?

✔ Did you use subject, object, and possessive pronouns correctly?

✔ Have you placed an apostrophe in each contraction?

39. Descriptive Adjectives

> **Adjectives** describe nouns or pronouns. Descriptive adjectives tell about the size, shape, color, weight, or other qualities of the things they describe. Some adjectives come before nouns.
>
> **courageous** firefighters   **messy** bedroom   **wonderful** aroma

A. Underline the descriptive adjectives in each sentence. The number in parentheses tells how many adjectives are in each sentence.

1. The early, golden sun shone on Sadako. (2)
2. It gave her dark hair brown highlights. (2)
3. She looked up at the clear sky. (1)
4. It was a good sign. (1)
5. Sadako went inside the small, neat house. (2)
6. She saw that her big brother was still asleep. (1)
7. "Get up, lazy one!" she said. (1)
8. The smell of delicious food filled the air. (1)
9. Hot eggs and crunchy toast awaited them in the kitchen. (2)
10. Sadako's sleepy brother dragged himself out of the comfortable bed. (2)

B. Complete each sentence with an adjective.

atomic	terrible	warm	crisp	Japanese
delicate	younger	soft	little	plain
awful	fresh	front	memorable	back

1. Helpful Sadako dressed her _____ brother Eiji.
2. She put the _____ blankets into the large closet.
3. In the kitchen her mother sliced _____ radishes.
4. This was a _____ day in Japan, August 6.
5. An _____ bomb fell on Hiroshima on this date in 1945.
6. Each year the _____ people remember those who died on that sad day.
7. Sadako's father came in from the _____ porch.
8. He called for everyone to gather near the _____ altar.
9. A small picture of an older woman was nearby in a _____ frame.
10. Sadako's great grandmother had died on that _____ day.

C. In addition to the adjectives that you have written on the lines, there are five other adjectives in the sentences in Part B. Circle them.

40. Proper Adjectives

Some descriptive adjectives come from proper nouns and are called **proper adjectives**. Proper adjectives begin with a capital letter.

PROPER NOUN   **Mexico**   **Sweden**

PROPER ADJECTIVE   **Mexican**   **Swedish**

Adjectives

A. Underline the proper adjective(s) in each sentence.

1. Ancient Olympic games were religious festivals.

2. Roman soldiers changed the festivals to contests.

3. The games disappeared from Western culture
   for 1,500 years.

4. A group of German archaeologists found stadium
   ruins in 1875.

5. A French educator organized the modern competition.

6. The Greek people hosted the first modern games.

7. The Winter Games have often been hosted by a European nation.

8. The first medal won by a woman went to a British woman in 1900.

9. Talented athletes from Scandinavian nations compete in winter sports.

10. American athletes make us proud in winter and summer competitions.

B. Complete each sentence with the adjective formed from the proper noun at the left.

America   1. The _____ diver scored a perfect 10.

Poland   2. The _____ runner finished the marathon in record time.

Russia   3. Dancing her way to fame, the _____ skater performed beautifully.

Cuba   4. The _____ players scored the winning point.

France   5. The _____ cyclists pedaled to the top of the velodrome.

Italy   6. One of the _____ relay runners dropped the baton.

Ireland   7. The _____ long-distance runner trained in America.

Egypt   8. In the floor exercise the _____ gymnast performed
             to modern music.

China   9. Despite the falling snow the _____ ski jumper outdistanced
             everyone.

Canada   10. The _____ basketball team lost by only one point.

Name _____

41. Articles

> *A, an,* and *the* are **articles**. *A* and *an* are **indefinite articles**. An indefinite article refers to any one of a class of things. *A* is used before words beginning with a consonant sound. *An* is used before words beginning with a vowel sound.
>
> **She ate a banana.**
> **An elephant eats enormous amounts of food.**
>
> *The* is the **definite article**. It refers to one or more specific things.
>
> **She ate the banana that was in the bowl.**
> **The elephants at the sanctuary eat tons of food each day.**

Underline the definite and indefinite articles below.

Father Damien was born in the town of Tremeloo, Belgium, on the third of January, 1840. His name then was Joseph de Vesteur. Joseph went to school at a college in Braine-le-Comte. He decided to become a priest and entered an order called the Fathers of the Sacred Heart of Jesus and Mary. At this time he took the name Damien.

Damien was given the assignment of doing mission work in Hawaii. Damien took on the job with great passion. He worked with the natives of the Hawaiian Islands, and he built a number of chapels with his own hands. He is best known for being a missionary to people with Hansen's disease, or leprosy, in the settlement on the island of Molokai. This work showed great courage because leprosy is a contagious disease. Damien ministered to the people, who had no doctors or nurses to care for them. He did this in the ways he could, by helping them build houses, by dressing their sores, by comforting them, and even by digging their graves. Father Damien ministered to these sick people until he himself contracted leprosy and died.

Father Damien helped people who had no one else to take care of them. Think of a person who needs care and attention. Give an example of how you can help that person.

42. Repetition of Articles

When two or more nouns joined by *and* name different people, places, or things, use an article before each noun. When two or more nouns joined by *and* refer to the same person, place, or thing, use an article before the first noun only.

The art teacher and the math teacher are in the gym. (more than one person)
The English teacher and drama coach is setting up the stage. (one person)

A. If the italicized phrase refers to one person, write **1**. If it refers to more than one person, write **+**.

_____ 1. *A composer and a lyricist* wrote the fifth-grade show.

_____ 2. *The producer and the director* selected the cast.

_____ 3. *The costume designer and set decorator* made everything look great.

_____ 4. *The singer, the actress, and the dancer* practiced every day.

_____ 5. *The actor and comedian* was late for rehearsal.

B. For each pair of sentences, read the first sentence to determine the article(s) needed in the second sentence. If no article is needed, put an **X** on the line.

1. Two people built the set. _____ set designer and _____ carpenter worked on it over the weekend.

2. One student did the publicity. _____ writer and _____ illustrator made posters.

3. One teacher provided props. _____ science teacher and _____ baseball coach lent bats and gloves to the cast.

4. Several students played instruments. _____ lead guitarist, _____ bass player, and _____ drummer rehearsed in the music room.

5. One person helped the actors. _____ makeup artist and _____ hairstylist helped the performers get ready.

C. Complete the paragraph with articles. If no article is needed, put an **X** on the line. More than one article can be used in some cases.

_____ musical *Wicked* is _____ story of _____ good witch,
    1.   2.   3.
Galinda, and _____ wicked witch, Elphaba. _____ composer and
            4.   5.
_____ lyricist, Stephen Schwartz, and _____ writer, Winnie Holzman,
    6.   7.
tell how _____ girls meet and become roommates at Shiz University.
        8.
_____ pretty Galinda and _____ green-skinned Elphaba are enemies
    9.   10.
who become best friends. _____ villain is Madame Morrible, _____
        11.   12.
sorcery teacher and _____ press secretary to the Wizard. What really
        13.
happened when Dorothy was blown to Oz by _____ tornado? _____
        14.   15.
answer this musical gives may surprise you!

Adjectives

43. Demonstrative Adjectives

> The **demonstrative adjectives** are *this, that, these,* and *those.*
> *This* and *that* point out one person, place, or thing.
>
> **this** skater   **that** judge
>
> *These* and *those* point out more than one person, place, or thing.
>
> **these** skaters   **those** judges
>
> *This* and *these* name persons, places, or things that are near.
>
> **this** costume next to me   **these** skates in my hand
>
> *That* and *those* name persons, places, or things that are far.
>
> **that** costume in the closet   **those** skates on the shelf

A. Circle the correct demonstrative adjective in parentheses.

1. In pair skating (this these) two compete regularly.
2. (That Those) skating outfit is a beautiful color.
3. The sequins on (that those) blouses glitter in the lights.
4. Having matching outfits makes (that those) pair look stylish.
5. (This These) pair of skates matches the sequined outfit perfectly.
6. For jumps on the ice, (these this) skates have toe picks.
7. (That Those) couple does ice dancing.
8. In their routine (that those) skaters can't do lifts.
9. Fast-moving music keeps (this these) two skating quickly.
10. (This These) type of skating looks like ballroom dancing.

B. Complete each sentence with the correct demonstrative adjective.

1. Figure skaters use _____ (*near*) type of skate.
2. _____ (*near*) skates have teeth cut in the front of the blade.
3. Spins and figures are made with _____ (*near*) toe picks.
4. Also, the bottoms of _____ (*near*) skates are curved.
5. _____ (*far*) skate is used just for speed skating.
6. _____ (*far*) skate boots are inexpensive and lightweight.
7. Steel tubing reinforces _____ (*far*) thin, flat blades.
8. The blades and boots on _____ (*far*) skates are designed for speed.
9. _____ (*near*) ice-hockey skates have very heavy boots.
10. Players get support and protection from _____ (*far*) shoe.

44. Adjectives That Tell How Many

Some adjectives tell how many or about how many.

SINGULAR		PLURAL	
10th inning	either man	six games	most exams
each athlete	little time	all mice	few boxes
neither boy	much popcorn	both knees	many smiles
every girl	any child	some days	any efforts
another runner		several movies	

A. Underline the adjectives that tell how many. Do not include articles.

1. The pentathlon is a competition of five events.

2. The events are held in one day.

3. The first event is the long jump.

4. Throwing the javelin is the second test.

5. Before throwing the javelin, the athlete takes several steps.

6. Each athlete must also throw a discus.

7. A discus is a round metal or wooden object weighing four pounds.

8. An athlete holds it in one hand and spins around before releasing it.

9. A decathlon has 10 events.

10. It is held over a period of two days.

B. Complete each sentence with an adjective that tells how many. Do not include articles.

1. The Winter Olympics are held every _____ years.

2. A gold medal is the _____ prize.

3. The _____ prize is a silver medal.

4. A bronze medal is given as a _____ prize.

5. There are _____ rings on the Olympic flag.

6. _____ countries have representative athletes.

7. _____ athletes are proud just to be there.

8. _____ members of teams receive individual medals.

9. _____ country should be proud of its athletes.

10. _____ athletes and coaches march in the parade.

45. Position of Adjectives

> An adjective usually comes before the noun it modifies.
>
> <u>delicate</u> flower   <u>shiny</u> penny
>
> When an adjective follows a linking verb, it is a subject complement. It completes the meaning of the verb and describes the subject of the sentence.
>
> **The flower is <u>delicate</u>.**   **The penny was <u>shiny</u>.**

A. Underline the descriptive adjectives.

1. A thick mitt helps the catcher.

2. Thinner gloves are used by the fielders.

3. The strong mask protects the face of the catcher.

4. The outfielder runs carefully on the wet grass.

5. The gloves are made from genuine leather.

B. Underline the subject complement in each sentence.

1. The catcher's mitt is thick.

2. Fielders' gloves are thinner.

3. The catcher's mask is strong.

4. The grass is wet.

5. The leather in baseball gloves is genuine.

C. Underline the adjectives that come before nouns.
Circle the subject complements.

1. The old baseball was dirty and worn.

2. The thread around the corky center is blue and gray.

3. Under the thread the black and red material is rubbery.

4. The leathery cover is smooth.

5. The precious signature on it is blurry.

Adjectives

46. Adjectives That Compare

The **positive** degree of an adjective shows a quality of a noun. The **comparative** degree is used to compare two items or two sets of items. It is often used with *than*. Many comparatives are formed by adding *-r* or *-er* to the positive. The **superlative** degree is used to compare three or more items. Many superlatives are formed by adding *-st* or *-est* to the positive. *Good* and *bad* have irregular forms of comparison.

POSITIVE	COMPARATIVE	SUPERLATIVE
Tom is tall.	Tom is taller than Jim.	Tom is the tallest boy.
Joe is thin.	Joe is thinner than Tom.	Joe is the thinnest boy.
Jim was happy.	Jim was happier than Joe.	Jim was the happiest boy.
Tom is a bad runner.	Jim is a worse runner.	Joe is the worst runner of all.

A. Write **P** if the phrase is positive, **C** if it is comparative, or **S** if it is superlative.

1. _____ loudest yell

2. _____ hard jab

3. _____ latest class

4. _____ tiny child

5. _____ fastest runner

6. _____ higher kick

7. _____ wise choice

8. _____ smoothest move

9. _____ whiter robe

10. _____ quicker punch

B. Complete each sentence with the adjective in the correct degree of comparison.

1. early *(superlative)* Karate is one of the _____ forms of unarmed combat.

2. close *(superlative)* "Empty hand" is the _____ translation for the Japanese *kara te*.

3. fast *(comparative)* Kung fu, Chinese karate, is _____ than karate and uses circular motions.

4. strong *(comparative)* Tae kwon do, Korean karate, uses _____, linear movements than other forms.

5. safe *(superlative)* The _____ use of karate is for self-defense.

6. good *(positive)* Karate is a _____ sport for children.

7. good *(comparative)* Most karate students have _____ balance and coordination than other children.

8. good *(superlative)* Karate is one of the _____ ways to build self-confidence.

9. low *(superlative)* The color of the belt for the _____ level in karate is white.

10. high *(superlative)* Students at the _____ level earn black belts.

Adjectives

47. More, Most and Less, Least

> Most adjectives of three or more syllables and some adjectives of two syllables do not add -er or -est to form the comparative and superlative degrees. Instead, the comparative is formed by adding *more* or *less* before the positive. The superlative is formed by adding *most* or *least* before the positive.
>
> I am intelligent.   They were careless.
> You are more intelligent than I.   They are less careless than you.
> They are the most intelligent students. She is least careless of all the girls.

A. Write the comparative and superlative of each adjective. Use *more* and *most.*

1. healthful _____   _____

2. tolerant _____   _____

3. dangerous _____   _____

4. beneficial _____   _____

5. nutritious _____   _____

B. Write the comparative and superlative of each adjective. Use *less* and *least.*

1. successful _____   _____

2. confident _____   _____

3. informative _____   _____

4. traditional _____   _____

5. original _____   _____

C. Choose the correct adjective to complete each sentence.

1. Insects are the (more numerous most numerous) creatures on earth.

2. Some kinds of insects are (more destructive most destructive) than others.

3. The (more harmful most harmful) insects eat crops or cause disease.

4. Predators and pollinators are the (more important most important) beneficial insects.

5. Ladybugs eat aphids, the (more common most common) plant pests.

6. Ladybug larvae are (less ferocious least ferocious) than they look.

7. Robber flies are (less common least common) than beetles.

8. Robber flies are also (more deadly most deadly) than many other insects.

9. Insects that pollinate flowers are the (more valuable most valuable) insects of all.

10. Honeybees are probably (more beneficial most beneficial) of all insects.

48. Fewer, Fewest and Less, Least

> *Fewer, fewest, less,* and *least* are used to compare things. Use *fewer* and *fewest* with plural count nouns. Use *less* and *least* with noncount nouns. Use *fewer* and *less* to compare two things or two sets of things. Use *fewest* and *least* to compare more than two things or sets of things.
>
> **COMPARATIVE**   **SUPERLATIVE**
> This recipe requires <u>fewer carrots</u>.   That recipe requires the <u>fewest carrots</u>.
> It requires <u>less celery</u> too.   It also requires the <u>least celery</u>.

Adjectives

A. Use *less* or *fewer* to write a phrase with each noun. The first one is done for you.

1. corn _____less corn_____   6. radishes _____

2. cherries _____   7. milk _____

3. beef _____   8. lemonade _____

4. bananas _____   9. ice cream _____

5. cookies _____   10. crackers _____

B. Write a phrase with each noun and *least* or *fewest*. The first one is done for you.

1. children ___fewest children___   6. paint _____

2. songs _____   7. music _____

3. laughter _____   8. tears _____

4. attention _____   9. pencils _____

5. women _____   10. dirt _____

C. Circle the correct word to complete each sentence.

1. Deserts get (less fewer) rain than other places on earth.

2. (Less Fewer) kinds of plants live in deserts than in places that are more temperate.

3. (Less Fewer) large mammals live in deserts than in other habitats.

4. There is (less fewer) food for them to eat in the desert.

5. There are also (less fewer) places for them to find shelter.

6. Hot, dry deserts get the (least fewest) precipitation.

7. They have the most heat and the (least fewest) humidity of all deserts.

8. The Atacama Desert in Chile gets the (least fewest) inches of rain of any desert.

9. Cold deserts have (less fewer) warm days than hot, dry deserts.

10. They have (less fewer) rainstorms and more snowfall.

49. More on *Fewer, Fewest* and *Less, Least*

> Use *fewer* and *fewest* with plural count nouns. Use *less* and *least*
> with noncount nouns. Remember that some nouns can be either
> count or noncount, depending on how they are used.
>
> **Mom prepared <u>fewer soups</u> this week than she did last week.
> She eats <u>less soup</u> than anyone in the family.**

A. Complete each sentence with *fewer* or *less*.

1. A healthful diet might include more whole grains and _____ white bread.

2. Eat more fruits and vegetables and _____ sugary snacks.

3. Salads with _____ salad dressing can be full of flavor.

4. Drink more water and _____ soft drinks.

5. A proper diet can result in _____ body fat.

6. Popcorn can be a good snack if it is made with _____ salt and butter.

7. Orange juice contains _____ fiber than whole oranges.

8. Fresh vegetables fill you up with _____ calories than many other foods.

9. Many vegetarians eat _____ fat than nonvegetarians.

10. People with food allergies may have _____ choices than other people.

B. Complete each sentence with *fewest* or *least*.

1. I have the _____ strange eating habits of anyone in my family.

2. My mom drinks the _____ milk of us all.

3. My sister eats the _____ meat.

4. My dad eats the _____ pieces of fruit each day.

5. My brother drinks the _____ glasses of juice.

6. Aunt Jody enjoys the _____ kinds of dessert.

7. My cousin Harry eats the _____ chocolate.

8. Uncle Norm drinks the _____ soft drinks.

9. Grandpa likes the _____ kinds of vegetables.

10. Grandma uses the _____ salt.

50. Interrogative Adjectives

An **interrogative adjective** is used in asking a question. The interrogative adjectives are *what, which,* and *whose.* An interrogative adjective comes before a noun. *What* is used for asking about people or things. *Which* is used to ask about one of two or more people or things. *Whose* asks about possession.

What kinds of animals live in coral reefs?
Which coral reef have you visited?
Whose job is it to protect coral reefs?

A. Circle the interrogative adjective in each sentence. Underline the noun it goes with.

1. What animals live in coral reefs?

2. Which type of coral has a limestone skeleton?

3. Which reef is the largest?

4. Whose report on coral reefs was most informative?

5. What organizations are involved in saving the reefs?

6. What habitats are in danger because of overfishing?

7. What species are in danger of becoming extinct?

8. Whose book on coral reefs did you read?

9. What action can you take to save the reefs?

10. To which politician will you write a letter?

B. Complete the sentence with a correct interrogative adjective. More than one choice may be correct.

1. To _____ group of animals do corals belong?

2. _____ types of fish have no bones, only cartilage?

3. _____ threats are there to coral reefs today?

4. _____ diagram of a sponge is most accurate?

5. _____ sea creatures have eight arms?

6. _____ tiny organisms do whales eat?

7. _____ favorite fish is the angel shark?

8. _____ reptiles usually live in a reef?

9. _____ video on turtles was most educational?

10. _____ turn is it to feed the fish?

Name _____

51. Reviewing Adjectives

A. **Complete the paragraph by writing the appropriate adjectives on the lines.**

spicy	juicy	fresh	crisp	creamy
flaky	cold	crunchy	hot	delicious

Athletes from various countries sat together and ate a _____ meal.
1.

They began with a _____ salad and a _____ fruit cup with a
2.   3.

_____ sauce. They shared _____ pizza slices, _____
4.   5.   6.

hamburgers, tacos in _____ shells, and _____ baked potatoes.
7.   8.

Picking only one of the _____ French pastries was difficult. The athletes
9.

seemed to drink gallons of _____ milk. Friendships were formed during
10.

this meal.

B. **Write the proper adjective for each type of food.**

11. _____ spaghetti (Italy)

12. _____ waffles (Belgium)

13. _____ pastries (France)

14. _____ chop suey (China)

15. _____ potato salad (Germany)

16. _____ sausage (Poland)

17. _____ enchiladas (Mexico)

18. _____ fondue (Switzerland)

19. _____ sushi (Japan)

20. _____ goulash (Hungary)

C. **Complete each sentence with the correct article.**

21. _____ athlete must eat a balanced diet.

22. _____ balanced diet is important to his or her training.

23. Eating correctly provides your body with _____ energy to compete.

24. She always eats _____ piece of fruit as a snack.

25. _____ fruit gives her a lot of energy.

CONTINUED

D. Complete each sentence with the correct demonstrative adjective (*this, that, these, those*).

26. "_____ (*near*) apples look good," thought Sadako.

27. She'd like a slice of _____ (*far*) watermelon.

28. Her brother wants some of _____ (*far*) cherries.

29. _____ (*near*) cantaloupe smells ripe.

30. _____ (*far*) grapes look delicious.

E. On the line write **P** if the *italicized* adjective is positive degree, **C** if it is comparative degree, or **S** if it is superlative degree.

_____ 31. Sadako believed in signs of *good* luck.

_____ 32. She looked forward to a *great* race.

_____ 33. Her *older* brother encouraged her.

_____ 34. He said she would be the *fastest* runner.

_____ 35. Sadako knew she was *better* than she had been last year.

F. Complete each sentence with a subject complement.

36. Sadako was _____ before the race.

37. Her legs were _____ but powerful.

38. When she won, Sadako was _____.

39. Her friends were _____ of her.

40. "Sadako always was _____," said her father.

Try It Yourself

Write three sentences about your favorite meal. Be sure to use adjectives correctly.

_____

_____

_____

Check Your Own Work

Choose a selection from your writing portfolio, your journal, a work in progress, an assignment from another class, or a letter. Revise it, applying the skills you have reviewed. This checklist will help you.

✔ Have you capitalized all proper adjectives?

✔ Have you used *a* and *an* correctly?

✔ Do your demonstrative adjectives agree in number with their nouns?

✔ Have you used each adjective in the correct degree?

52. Action Verbs—Part I

> An **action verb** is a word used to express action.
> Tom <u>opened</u> his birthday presents.

A. Circle the action verb in each sentence.

1. Bobby studies every day after school.

2. Sometimes he works on a project with a friend.

3. Yesterday his science teacher gave the class an assignment.

4. Bobby visited his new friend John.

5. The boys performed the science experiment.

6. John went to the kitchen for a snack.

7. He returned with two glasses of lemonade.

8. Then the kitchen door opened again.

9. John entered with some cookies.

10. But John already stood beside Bobby with the lemonade!

B. Complete each sentence with an action verb.

1. Bobby _____ in astonishment.

2. He _____ from one boy to the other.

3. He _____ his hand in front of his eyes.

4. He _____ he must have studied too long.

5. Sometimes your eyes _____ tricks on you.

6. Bobby _____ to his feet.

7. John _____ that the second boy was his twin.

8. He _____ Bobby and Jason.

9. Bobby _____ at their joke.

10. "You _____ me!" he said.

53. Action Verbs—Part II

A. Complete each sentence with an action verb.

1. The Joyces _____ to the animal shelter to get a dog.

2. The puppy _____ its tail when it saw the children.

3. Claire _____ the dog Coco.

4. Sean _____ a bed for the puppy.

5. Sean and Claire _____ turns feeding Coco.

6. Sean _____ the puppy after school every day.

7. Yesterday he _____ with Coco at the park.

8. There Coco _____ a hole to bury her toy.

9. She always _____ at strangers.

10. Coco _____ on socks if they are on the floor.

11. Sometimes she _____ a squirrel up a tree.

12. Coco _____ Claire every morning by tugging the blankets.

13. Clair _____ Coco a ball.

14. Coco _____ it every time!

15. At the end of the day, Coco _____ in her own bed.

B. Write a sentence, using each verb.

giggle   1. _____

tumble   2. _____

ride   3. _____

play   4. _____

jog   5. _____

grasp   6. _____

scream   7. _____

tickle   8. _____

jump   9. _____

nap   10. _____

Verbs

54. Action Verbs—Part III

A. Write an action verb that each group of people or things can perform.

1. puppies _____
2. birds _____
3. children _____
4. students _____
5. rock stars _____
6. authors _____
7. babies _____
8. athletes _____
9. cows _____
10. boats _____

11. flowers _____
12. horses _____
13. cars _____
14. balloons _____
15. clocks _____
16. tires _____
17. bunnies _____
18. fish _____
19. dishes _____
20. windows _____

B. Complete each sentence with a verb from the list. Use each word once.

cried	yelled	asked	whispered	responded
called	questioned	exclaimed	shouted	replied

1. "Oh no!" _____ Molly.

2. "My rabbit's cage door is open, and he's gone!"

   she _____.

3. She _____ for her sister.

4. "Have you seen Fluffy?" _____ Molly.

5. Hannah _____, "No, but I'll help you find him."

6. They _____, "Fluffy, come here, Fluffy."

7. After looking for hours, Hannah _____,
   "There he is, sleeping!"

8. "How sweet!" Molly _____ so she wouldn't wake him.

9. "What should we do?" _____ Hannah.

10. Molly _____, "Let's let him sleep."

55. Being Verbs

> A **being verb** is a word used to express existence. The most common being verbs are *is, are, was, were, be, been,* and *being.*

A. Circle the being verb in each sentence. If the being verb has a helping verb, circle the entire verb.

1. Traveling is a lot of fun.
2. I have been on many trips.
3. My trip to Utah was incredible.
4. We were alone in the desert under millions of stars.
5. The many stars were our tiny personal lanterns.
6. I have been to several U.S. national parks.
7. The hiking trails will be open soon in Grand Teton National Park.
8. The trails were not open last fall because of the snow.
9. It has been a long time since I have hiked in the mountains.
10. I hear that you will be in Rome soon.
11. Rome has been a religious site for centuries.
12. There are so many beautiful churches there.
13. The Vatican Museum is full of famous works by Michelangelo and Raphael.
14. The Sistine Chapel ceiling has been famous for centuries.
15. There are many wonderful countries, cities, and landscapes to see and explore.

B. Underline the being verbs in the paragraph.

Venice has been a major Italian city for centuries. There are few streets in Venice, but there are many canals. The biggest one is the Grand Canal. It has been the "Main Street" of Venice for a long time. The center of activity is St. Mark's Square. This is a large area near St. Mark's Cathedral. People will be there even late at night. In Venice, boats are the chief means of transportation. The gondola is a famous kind of Venetian boat. Its movement is from an oar controlled by a gondolier. Gondoliers have been the operators of these boats for centuries. Today gondolas are mainly for tourists. Boats with motors are more common now. Venice will always be an interesting and unusual city to visit.

Verbs

Name _____

56. Verb Phrases

> A **verb phrase** is a group of words that does the work of a single verb. A verb phrase contains one or more helping verbs (*is, are, has, have, do, will, can, could, would, should,* and so on) and a main verb.
>
> **Regular exercise <u>is needed</u> for good health.**
> **He <u>could have improved</u> his health by hiking.**

Underline the verb phrase in each sentence. Write on the lines the helping verb(s) and the main verb.

	HELPING VERB	MAIN VERB
1. In the spring he will hike the Appalachian Trail.	_____	_____
2. The Appalachian Trail is also called the A.T.	_____	_____
3. Hiking the trail from end to end is called thru-hiking.	_____	_____
4. A thru-hiker will cross about 2,100 miles.	_____	_____
5. The trail has been marked with blazes.	_____	_____
6. White rectangular marks have been painted on trees.	_____	_____
7. Blazes can keep hikers from becoming lost.	_____	_____
8. Hikers should make camp before sundown.	_____	_____
9. On the A.T. a camper can find shelters a day's hike apart.	_____	_____
10. Many people have camped along the trail.	_____	_____
11. Porcupines are sighted near some campsites.	_____	_____
12. Black bears have appeared along the trail.	_____	_____
13. Campers should leave no trace after using a campsite.	_____	_____
14. You should visit the A.T. once in your lifetime.	_____	_____
15. Thousands of people will hike the trail this year.	_____	_____

57. More Verb Phrases

In questions and negative statements the helping verb and the main verb may be separated.

<u>Will</u> you <u>come</u> to the party tonight?   **They <u>are</u> not <u>expected</u> to be there.**

A. Underline the main verb and the helping verb in each sentence.

1. Do you like dogs?
2. Carlos does not own a dog.
3. Do Dalmatians have spots?
4. Has Frisky been to the veterinarian yet?
5. Frisky did not enjoy the vaccination.
6. Can Great Danes grow that tall?
7. Was Frisky walked after school?
8. My dog does not bark often.
9. Poodles do not shed much.
10. Did Bandit dig that hole in the yard?
11. What do English foxhounds like to hunt?
12. Can your dog jump over the fence?
13. Do you brush your Old English sheepdog often in the summer?
14. Can your Saint Bernard fit through the door?
15. Were chows used for hunting?

B. Answer each question with a negative response. Underline the main verb and the helping verb in the question and the response.

1. Did you watch the late movie last night?

   _____

2. May she go to the movies tonight?

   _____

3. Should we watch the film at nine o'clock?

   _____

4. Will he buy popcorn for the show?

   _____

5. Are they paying for the show themselves?

   _____

Verbs

58. Principal Parts of Verbs

A verb has four **principal parts: present, present participle, past,** and **past participle.** The present participle of verbs is formed by adding *-ing* to the present part. For verbs ending in *e,* drop the final *e* before adding *-ing.* The present participle is used with forms of the helping verb *be (am, is, are, was, were, been).*

> jump   jumping   scrape   scraping   tap   tapping

The past and the past participle of regular verbs is formed by adding *-d* or *-ed* to the present part. For verbs ending in *y* following a consonant, change the *y* to *i* before adding *-ed.* The past participle is used with the helping verb *have (has, had).*

> jump   jumped   scrape   scraped   fry   fried

For single-syllable verbs that end with a consonant following a vowel, double the final consonant before adding *-ing* or *-ed.*

> step   stepping   stepped

A. Write the present participle, the past, and the past participle of each verb.

	PRESENT PARTICIPLE	PAST	PAST PARTICIPLE
1. cheer	_____	_____	_____
2. sigh	_____	_____	_____
3. play	_____	_____	_____
4. laugh	_____	_____	_____
5. walk	_____	_____	_____
6. roll	_____	_____	_____
7. yell	_____	_____	_____
8. sneeze	_____	_____	_____
9. hop	_____	_____	_____
10. crawl	_____	_____	_____

B. Write a sentence, using the direction in parentheses and the verb *jump.*

1. (Use the past tense.) _____
2. (Use the present tense.) _____
3. (Use the present participle.) _____
4. (Use the past tense.) _____
5. (Use the past participle.) _____

Verbs

59. Regular and Irregular Verbs

> The past and past participle of regular verbs end in *-ed* or *-d.*
> The past and past participles of **irregular verbs** do not end in -ed or -d.

A. Underline the verb or verb phrase in each sentence. Write **R** on the line if the principal verb is regular or **I** if it is irregular.

_____ 1. Recently our class took a trip to the Vietnam War Memorial.

_____ 2. The memorial is located in Washington, D.C.

_____ 3. It was built in honor of those who served in Vietnam.

_____ 4. The names of all the dead were carved in stone.

_____ 5. Family members and friends have often visited the memorial.

_____ 6. Some found the name of deceased loved ones.

_____ 7. Often they left flowers at the site.

_____ 8. The flowers were a sign of remembrance.

_____ 9. The memorial has made a lasting impression on each visitor.

_____ 10. We have learned to appreciate the sacrifices of those who served.

B. Write a sentence, using each verb in the past tense. Write **R** on the line if the verb is regular or **I** if it is irregular.

_____ 1. buy _____

_____ 2. eat _____

_____ 3. laugh _____

_____ 4. walk _____

_____ 5. study _____

_____ 6. make _____

_____ 7. answer _____

_____ 8. know _____

_____ 9. paint _____

_____ 10. talk _____

Verbs

Name _____

60. More Regular and Irregular Verbs

A. Complete each sentence with the simple past or the past participle of the verb. Remember to use the past participle if the sentence has a helping verb.

fall   1. How much rain _____ here last year?

study   2. Scientists have _____ rainfall for years.

collect   3. The rain is _____ in a bucket.

stop   4. When the rain has _____, the scientists measure the depth.

make   5. They have _____ studies of the weather cycle from the results.

be   6. Rain has always _____ an important source of fresh water.

cause   7. Today air pollutants have _____ some rainwater to be unhealthful.

result   8. Many human activities have also _____ in polluted water.

find   9. Polluted water has been _____ to be dangerous to human health.

learn   10. We _____ that polluted water can make us sick.

B. Complete each sentence with the simple past or the past participle of the verb.

eat   1. Mike had _____ his breakfast early that day.

grow   2. The plant _____ two inches.

give   3. I had _____ my catcher's mitt to my friend.

go   4. Who _____ to the game yesterday?

throw   5. The outfielder _____ the ball to the catcher.

teach   6. Our teacher had _____ us how to add fractions.

display   7. Harold _____ the population data in a circle graph.

try   8. We _____ that solution to the equation.

jump   9. The athlete _____ rope for exercise.

stand   10. Fans _____ in line for concert tickets.

Verbs

61. Am, Is, Are, Was, and Were

The present tense forms of the verb *be* are *am, is,* and *are.* The past tense forms are *was* and *were.* Use *am* with the first person singular pronoun *I.* Use *is* or *was* with a singular noun or the third person singular pronoun *he, she,* or *it.* Use *are* or *were* with a plural noun, the first person plural pronoun *we,* the second person pronoun *you,* or the third person plural pronoun *they.*

I <u>am</u> glad to be here.
You <u>are</u> a talented musician.
The <u>musicians</u> in the band <u>are</u> great.

I <u>was</u> here yesterday.
You <u>were</u> not here yet.
The <u>musicians</u> <u>were</u> on stage.

A. Circle the correct form of *be* in parentheses.

1. Minerals and vitamins (is are) some of the body's essential nutrients.

2. Some minerals (is are) present in the body in tiny, or trace, amounts.

3. Calcium (is are) important for the growth of bones.

4. Vitamins (is are) thought to promote health.

5. Vegetables (is are) good sources of vitamins.

B. Complete each sentence with *am, is,* or *are.*

1. Your friends _____ here.

2. What _____ the matter?

3. I _____ on the phone.

4. She _____ ready to go.

5. _____ you sure you want to leave now?

C. Circle the correct form of *be* in parentheses.

1. (Was Were) Jeff in the science lab with you?

2. He (was were) not in the lab yesterday.

3. The teacher (was were) quite helpful.

4. The students (was were) disappointed with the result.

5. The final exam (was were) difficult.

D. Complete each sentence with *was* or *were.*

1. The children _____ surprised.

2. The clowns _____ on tiny bikes.

3. The magician _____ in black.

4. The rabbit _____ in the magician's hat.

5. _____ you at the circus too?

Verbs

Name _____

62. Do, Does, Doesn't, and Don't

Use *does* or *doesn't* (*does not*) when the subject is a singular noun or a third person singular subject pronoun *(he, she, it)*.

> **The striped shirt <u>does</u> go with that plain skirt.**
> **He <u>doesn't</u> seem to have a lunch.**

Use *do* or *don't* (*do not*) when the subject is a plural noun or with the subject pronouns *I, we, you,* and *they*.

> **Motorists <u>do</u> like clearly marked street signs.**
> **We <u>don't</u> have the money to go on vacation right now.**

A. Circle the correct verb in parentheses.

1. This chair (does do) match the other chairs.

2. (Doesn't Don't) this striped velvet look good on it?

3. I (doesn't don't) usually like that material.

4. The couch (does do) look comfortable.

5. (Doesn't Don't) you like sitting on leather?

6. I (does do) like sitting on things that are soft.

7. Velvet (doesn't don't) look so bad to me now.

8. Why (doesn't don't) we try covering the couch with it?

9. (Does do) it cost a fortune?

10. Yes, because we (doesn't don't) get it wholesale.

B. Complete each sentence with *does* or *doesn't* or *do* or *don't*.

1. Those curtains _____ hang gracefully.

2. _____ they have ties to hold them back?

3. One tie _____ work.

4. _____ the living room look nice when the curtains are drawn?

5. The sun and the breeze _____ come in when the curtains are closed.

6. The room _____ look gloomy now.

7. _____ you think the room could use more color?

8. _____ that yellow pillow cheer things up?

9. One pillow _____ make the couch more comfortable.

10. _____ you want to buy some bright fabrics for this room?

63. Come and Go, Bring and Take

The verb *come* means "to move toward something." Its principal parts are *come, coming, came,* and *come.* The verb *go* means "to move away from a place." Its principal parts are *go, going, went,* and *gone.*

He <u>came</u> into the room with an armful of books.
Later he <u>went</u> out the side door to the gym.

The verb *bring* denotes action toward the speaker. Its principal parts are *bring, bringing, brought,* and *brought.* The verb *take* indicates an action toward another place. Its principal parts are *take, taking, took,* and *taken.*

<u>Bring</u> your math book to my house this evening.
You may <u>take</u> my camera on your field trip to the museum.

A. Circle the correct verb in parentheses.

1. Will you (take bring) this letter to the post office, please?

2. When you return, (take bring) some batteries from the hardware store.

3. Lou (took brought) his flashlight to my house, but the batteries were dead.

4. I wish he had (taken brought) me a flashlight with good batteries.

5. Will he be (taking bringing) the equipment to the gym tomorrow?

B. Circle the correct verb in parentheses.

1. Phil (comes goes) to that restaurant regularly.

2. You can see from across the street how many people (come go) into the restaurant.

3. My aunt plans to visit that restaurant when she (comes goes) to town to visit us.

4. I wish she would (come go) to visit soon because I enjoy her company.

5. After she has (come gone) to see all her other nephews, she will stop by our house.

**C. Write one sentence each, using the present participle of *take, bring, come,* and *go.*
Then write one sentence, using *take* in the past tense.**

1. _____

2. _____

3. _____

4. _____

5. _____

Verbs

Name _____

64. Sit and Set, Teach and Learn

> The verb *sit (sitting, sat, sat)* means "to have a place" or "to keep a seat."
> The verb *set (setting, set, set)* means "to place" or "to fix in position."
>
> **He <u>sat</u> there all day, staring into the distance.**
> **She <u>set</u> the clock on her nightstand and <u>set</u> it for five a.m.**
>
> The verb *teach (teaching, taught, taught)* means "to give instruction" or "to pass on knowledge." The verb *learn (learning, learned, learned)* means "to receive instruction or knowledge."
>
> **Ana <u>teaches</u> history to fifth graders.**
> **The children have <u>learned</u> a lot about the colonists.**

A. Circle the correct verb in parentheses.

1. We (sit set) the trophy on the top shelf.

2. I (sit set) across from my sister at the dinner table.

3. The dog (set sat) on the steps all morning.

4. My brother (sits sets) too close to the TV.

5. I (sat set) the glass next to the knife.

B. Complete each sentence with a correct form of *sit* or *set*.

1. Who _____ on the porch swing yesterday?

2. _____ here and rest for a while.

3. Where should I _____ the table?

4. Please _____ the table for dinner.

5. The baby _____ in her high chair.

C. Circle the correct verb in parentheses.

1. My grandfather (taught learned) me how to cook.

2. I (taught learned) to make meatloaf first.

3. Anyone who (teaches learns) someone must be patient.

4. My mother (taught learned) that I like to taste as I cook.

5. She (taught learned) me that cooking is an art.

D. Complete each sentence with a correct form of *teach* or *learn*.

1. Last year in school we _____ about sound.

2. This year we _____ about volcanoes.

3. Our math teacher last year _____ us how to divide.

4. Some students _____ long division very slowly.

5. I wish someone had _____ me French!

Name _____

65. Simple Tenses

The **tense of a verb** shows the time of its action. There are three simple tenses. The **simple present tense** tells about something that is always true or about an action that happens again and again. The **simple past tense** tells about an action that happened in the past. The **future tense** tells about an action that will happen.

SIMPLE PRESENT	The children <u>play</u> games at recess.
SIMPLE PAST	They <u>played</u> quietly for an hour.
FUTURE	They <u>are going to play</u> softball tomorrow.
	They <u>will leave</u> early.

Underline the verb or verb phrase in each sentence. Write the tense on the line.

_____ 1. Years after her death, Dorothea Dix still lives in history books.

_____ 2. Dorothea spent much of her life in Maine and Massachusetts.

_____ 3. She carried the heartache of an unhappy childhood.

_____ 4. Dorothea presents an image of a teacher in the early 1800s.

_____ 5. At age 14 she founded a school for young children.

_____ 6. Dorothea learned of the problems of people with mental illness.

_____ 7. She devoted her life to their care.

_____ 8. People with mental illness still need help today.

_____ 9. Where are they going to find this help?

_____ 10. She investigated jails' treatment of the mentally ill.

_____ 11. With a rich friend's help, Dorothea built a state hospital in New Jersey.

_____ 12. In Europe she educated nurses on patient care.

_____ 13. Because of Dorothea, nurses will continue the study of all aspects of patient care.

_____ 14. Only a very generous person volunteers to serve others.

_____ 15. Dorothea's epitaph describes her as the most useful and distinguished woman in America.

Dorothea Dix believed in helping people with physical and mental illnesses, so she fought for their rights. How can you serve others? Give an example.

Verbs

66. Subject-Verb Agreement

A subject and a verb always agree in number and person. If the subject is a third person singular noun or *he, she,* or *it,* add *-s* or *-es* to the end of the verb. Noncount nouns are always considered singular.

I eat breakfast every day.   The bus waits at the red light.
You wait for the bus at six o'clock.   She eats lunch in the cafeteria.
                                           The cat watches the mouse.

Plural nouns and the subject pronouns *we, you,* and *they* must always have verbs that do not add *-s* or *-es.*

Bikers observe traffic laws.
They carry their lunches with them.
We buy the same newspaper every day.

Verbs

Circle the correct verb form in parentheses. The subject is *italicized*.

1. Each year my *father* (visit visits) my grandparents in Ireland.

2. *He* (stay stays) two weeks each time.

3. *He* (take takes) along pictures of my brothers and me.

4. My *grandfather* (is are) always surprised by how much we've grown.

5. My *grandparents* (take takes) my father to see relatives.

6. *They* (has have) tea and sandwiches.

7. The *tea* (is are) made with milk and sugar.

8. My *grandmother* (know knows) many old Irish songs.

9. *She* (is are) always singing them.

10. My *grandparents* (has have) a dog named Shep.

11. My *grandfather* (walk walks) to the shore every morning.

12. *People* (is are) at work catching lobsters.

13. *Shep* (go goes) with my grandfather.

14. A *donkey* (is are) in their backyard.

15. My *father* always (bring brings) gifts from my grandparents.

67. Progressive Tenses

The **present progressive tense** tells what is happening now. The present progressive tense is formed with a present form of the verb *be (am, is, are)* and the present participle.

    He <u>is riding</u> his bike in the park.

The **past progressive tense** tells what was happening in the past. The past progressive tense is formed with a past form of the verb *be (was, were)* and the present participle.

    He <u>was riding</u> his bike when the accident happened.

The **future progressive tense** tells what will be happening in the future. The future progressive tense is formed with *will, is going to,* or *are going to* with *be* and the present participle.

    He <u>is going to be having</u> a cast put on his ankle.

Verbs

Underline the verb phrase in each sentence.
Write the tense on the line.

1. We are all having a great day. _____

2. The sun is shining. _____

3. Later we will be playing kick ball.

   _____

4. It was raining a while ago. _____

5. Trees were swaying in the strong wind. _____

6. Now I am strolling through the park. _____

7. Children are playing on the swings. _____

8. People are eating their lunches in the sunshine. _____

9. In the fall the sun will be setting much earlier. _____

10. Now everyone is enjoying the nice weather. _____

11. Yesterday at this time I was sitting in school. _____

12. The teacher was explaining the movements of planets. _____

13. They are all revolving around the sun. _____

14. They are also rotating on their axes. _____

15. Next week we will be studying cloud types. _____

68. Present Perfect Tense

> The **present perfect tense** tells about an action that happened at some indefinite time in the past or an action that started in the past and continues into the present time. The present perfect tense is formed with *have* or *has* and the past participle.
>
> **Alma <u>has made</u> potato salad for the reunion.**

A. **Underline the present perfect tense verb in each sentence.**

1. My mother's family has had a family reunion every summer for years.

2. My family has gone to the reunion since I was a baby.

3. We have enjoyed ourselves every time.

4. For the last five years the reunions have been at the local park.

5. Cousin Ona has won the sack race more times than I can count.

6. For years my uncles have been in charge of the grill.

7. Now the cousins have announced that they want to take over the job.

8. My grandmother has outdone herself this year.

9. She has made three piñatas!

10. We have already started the plans for next year's reunion.

B. **Complete each sentence with the present perfect tense of the verb.**

ask   1. Many eager fans _____ the star for her autograph.

try   2. She _____ to avoid them.

refuse   3. She _____ to leave her hotel room.

gather   4. Hundreds of people _____ on the sidewalk.

wait   5. They _____ patiently for hours.

make   6. Many of them _____ signs with her name.

speak   7. Her manager _____ to her several times.

urge   8. He _____ her to wave from the window.

arrive   9. A limousine _____ to take her to the awards ceremony.

tell   10. The driver _____ the fans to leave.

Name _____

69. Past Perfect Tense

> The **past perfect tense** tells about a past action that was completed before another past action started. The past perfect tense is formed with *had* and the past participle.
>
> **Seth <u>had eaten</u> three slices of ham before his mother got home.**

A. **Underline the past perfect tense verb in each sentence.**

1. In the 1800s scientists claimed they <u>had found</u> canals on Mars.
2. They said that space creatures <u>had dug</u> the canals.
3. People believed that life <u>had existed</u> on that planet.
4. The scientists <u>had seen</u> channels but not canals dug by living creatures.
5. The channels might prove that water <u>had been</u> there at some time in the past.
6. Long before humans sent out spacecraft, writers <u>had imagined</u> life on Mars.
7. By the 1890s H. G. Wells <u>had written</u> about an invasion of Earth by Martians.
8. Ray Bradbury's book *The Martian Chronicles* said that inhabitants of Earth <u>had invaded</u> Mars.
9. Before the Mars Rovers landed, no one <u>had known</u> what the planet was really like.
10. Scientists <u>had created</u> Martian conditions in a lab here before they tested a rover on Mars.

B. **Complete each sentence with the past perfect tense of the verb.**

think 1. Before the discoveries of Galileo Galilei, most people _____ that the sun revolved around the earth.

read 2. By the early 1600s Galileo _____ about telescopes.

make 3. Within a short time Galileo _____ his own telescope.

discover 4. After he _____ four of Jupiter's moons, Galileo looked at the Milky Way.

believe 5. Before Galileo learned that the Milky Way is made up of stars, scientists _____ that it was just a cloud.

observe 6. Galileo was the first European to discover sunspots, although Chinese astronomers _____ them much earlier.

focus 7. After he _____ his telescope on the moon, Galileo announced that the moon had mountains and craters.

conclude 8. By 1616 Galileo _____ that the earth revolves around the sun.

write 9. Some officials were angry because Galileo _____ that the earth moves.

publish 10. He was brought to trial because he _____ his views.

70. Future Perfect Tense

> The **future perfect tense** is used to talk about a future event that will be started and completed before another future event. The future perfect tense is formed with *will have* and the past participle.
>
> **We <u>will have eaten</u> lunch by the time the game starts.**

A. Underline the future perfect tense verb in each sentence.

1. By next month the students will have completed their projects for the science fair.

2. Bill and Henry will have chosen their project by the end of today.

3. By Monday Carla will have constructed her volcano.

4. Laura and Bryan will have designed their rocket by the end of the week.

5. Mr. Navarro will have mailed the applications by Friday.

6. Before his lettuce has sprouted, Vijay will have read about organic fertilizers.

7. Mia will have finished her model of the solar system by next Thursday.

8. By next week Keith will have collected all the materials he needs for his project.

9. By the time she's finished, Ann will have tried her experiment many times.

10. Everyone will have worked hard to finish on time.

B. Complete each sentence with the future perfect tense of the verb.

drive 1. By the end of the week, we _____ across South Dakota.

reach 2. By Monday afternoon we _____ the city of Mitchell.

visit 3. Before dinnertime we _____ the Corn Palace.

cross 4. By lunchtime on Tuesday we _____ the Missouri River.

drive 5. We _____ to the Badlands by Tuesday evening.

see 6. By Wednesday we _____ bison at Custer State Park.

explore 7. By Thursday night we _____ Jewel Cave.

stop 8. Before leaving Hot Springs, we _____ at Mammoth Site.

view 9. Before heading home, we _____ Mount Rushmore.

have 10. We hope that by then we _____ a great time.

71. Linking Verbs

A **linking verb** links, or joins, a subject with a subject complement, which identifies or describes the subject. The subject complement may be a noun, a pronoun, or an adjective. Verbs of being are linking verbs.

NOUN   She *is* the <u>teacher</u> of this class.
PRONOUN   The talented artist *was* <u>he</u>.
ADJECTIVE   The man behind the counter *was* <u>gruff</u>.

Verbs

A. Circle the subject complement in each sentence. Write on the line whether it is a noun, a pronoun, or an adjective. The linking verbs are *italicized*.

_____ 1. The orange *is* a fruit that contains vitamin C.

_____ 2. Those apples *are* green.

_____ 3. The fruit vendor *was* he.

_____ 4. Honeydew *is* the melon my mother likes least.

_____ 5. The rotten bananas *were* mushy.

_____ 6. These strawberries and blueberries *are* our dessert tonight.

_____ 7. Peaches *are* the main ingredient in this pie.

_____ 8. The best fruit-smoothie maker *is* she.

_____ 9. Those fresh apples *will be* cobbler when she is finished with them.

_____ 10. The pie-making contest *has* always *been* fun.

B. Complete each sentence with a subject complement. Use a noun, a pronoun, or an adjective.

1. The Art Institute of Chicago is a _____ that millions of people visit every year.

2. Monet and Picasso are _____ whose works hang in the Art Institute.

3. Water lilies have been the _____ of some of Monet's greatest paintings.

4. The water lilies are _____.

5. Was it not _____ who purchased the painting for a million dollars?

Name _____

72. Reviewing Verbs

A. Underline the verb in each sentence. Circle **A** if it is an action verb or **B** if it is a being verb.

1. We walked along the beach.   A   B

2. The sun was warm.   A   B

3. Waves lapped against the shore.   A   B

4. A seagull soared overhead.   A   B

5. We were happy to be there.   A   B

B. Underline the verb phrase in each sentence. Write the helping verb on the line.

_____ 6. Marie had run along the beach earlier.

_____ 7. Did she pass the hot dog stand?

_____ 8. She will buy a salad for lunch.

_____ 9. We might have salad for lunch too.

_____ 10. We can decide that later.

C. Write the principal parts of each verb.

	PRESENT PARTICIPLE	PAST	PAST PARTICIPLE
11. break	_____	_____	_____
12. call	_____	_____	_____
13. make	_____	_____	_____
14. choose	_____	_____	_____
15. go	_____	_____	_____

D. Circle the correct verb in parentheses.

16. (Bring Take) the map with you when you leave.

17. Friends at the party said Myrna had left and had (gone come) home.

18. Will you (bring take) refreshments when you come here for the meeting?

19. I (brought took) the audio equipment from the storeroom over to the gym.

20. When Kyle (comes goes) on the next field trip, he should wear sunglasses.

E. Circle the linking verb or verb phrase. Underline the subject complement and write **N** if it is a noun, **A** if it is an adjective, or **P** if it is a pronoun.

21. The boys are almost identical.   _____

22. Perhaps the first boy was John.   _____

23. The second boy looks taller.   _____

24. I think the second boy is he.   _____

25. The first boy could be his cousin.   _____

F. What is the tense of the underlined verb in each sentence? Write *present, past, future, present progressive, past progressive, future progressive, present perfect, past perfect,* or *future perfect* on the line. Not all tenses are used.

_____ 26. Pelicans <u>live</u> on every continent except Antarctica.

_____ 27. Scientists <u>have found</u> pelican fossils almost 40 million years old.

_____ 28. I <u>had</u> often <u>watched</u> pelicans on trips to the beach.

_____ 29. A soaring brown pelican <u>spied</u> a fish far below in the water.

_____ 30. Seconds later the bird <u>was plunging</u> rapidly toward its prey.

_____ 31. The bird <u>scooped</u> the fish into its large beak.

_____ 32. Pelicans <u>live</u> very long lives.

_____ 33. Scientists found one bird that they <u>had banded</u> more than 30 years earlier.

_____ 34. <u>Will</u> these birds <u>become</u> extinct?

_____ 35. I hope I <u>will be watching</u> pelicans for a long time.

Try It Yourself
Write four sentences about something funny or amazing that happened to you. Be sure to use verbs correctly.

_____

_____

_____

_____

Check Your Own Work
Choose a selection from your writing portfolio, your journal, a work in progress, an assignment from another class, or a letter. Revise it, applying the skills you have reviewed. This checklist will help you.

✔ Have you used the correct forms of irregular verbs?

✔ Have you used the correct tenses?

✔ Do your subjects agree with your verbs in person and number?

Name _____

73. Adverbs of Time

An **adverb** modifies a verb, an adjective, or another adverb.

> **He ran swiftly.** (modifies verb *ran*)
> **She is extremely intelligent.** (modifies adjective *intelligent*)
> **My father spoke quite sternly to me.** (modifies adverb *sternly*)

Adverbs of time answer the question *when* or *how often*. Some adverbs of time are *again, already, always, before, early, finally, frequently, now, often, soon, today,* and *yesterday.*

A. Underline the adverb in each sentence that tells *when* or *how often*.

1. Miriam told me a story yesterday.

2. I had not heard it before.

3. Today she promised to tell me two more.

4. First an African tale will be presented.

5. Who knows what will happen next!

6. Once there lived a very poor couple.

7. They were usually dressed in rags.

8. They had no children, but they often wished for some.

9. They always hoped for a better future.

10. Sometimes they dreamed about what might happen.

B. Circle the adverb of time in each sentence and write it on the line.

_____ 1. The poor man once met a man named Abinuku.

_____ 2. They soon became friends.

_____ 3. Abinuku was seldom happy or content.

_____ 4. He usually held much hate in his heart.

_____ 5. The poor man seldom knew Abinuku's true feelings.

_____ 6. The poor man frequently prayed for a better life.

_____ 7. Help was finally promised to him.

_____ 8. Often Money, Child, and Patience would visit him.

_____ 9. He would then have to choose which gift to keep.

_____ 10. How could he ever choose?

74. Adverbs of Place

> **Adverbs of place** answer the question *where*.
>
> **The farmer fell <u>backward</u> into the haystack.**
> (Where did the farmer fall? He fell *backward*.)
>
> Some adverbs of place are *above, away, backward, below,*
> *down, forth, here, in, out, there,* and *up*.

A. Underline the adverb in each sentence that tells *where*.

1. We stood there on the busiest corner.

2. My mother shops here.

3. We looked upward to the top of the new mall.

4. Someone decided it was time to go forward and shop.

5. I would go in if I had money.

6. She took the escalator down to the floor with the shoe stores.

7. The salesperson walked away from the counter.

8. My mother's friend walked on as we tried a new computer.

9. They all met inside to have lunch.

10. I walked ahead toward the movie theater.

B. Complete each sentence with an adverb of place.

1. You will find the athletes _____, near the locker room.

2. They won't come _____ before they stretch.

3. Their fans gather _____ at Wimbledon.

4. Tennis professionals like playing _____.

5. Two players walk _____ toward the court.

6. The judges come _____ and greet them, wishing them both luck.

7. The line judge stands _____ to observe the line.

8. A player runs _____ to the net.

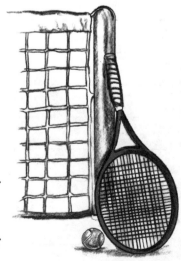

9. The camera crew moves _____ when the player approaches them.

10. The winner walks _____ from the match with a trophy and a smile.

Name _____

75. Adverbs of Manner

> **Adverbs of manner** answer the question *how*.
>
> **The contestant spelled the word <u>correctly</u>.**
> (How did the contestant spell the word?
> The contestant spelled it *correctly*.)
>
> Some adverbs of manner are *carefully, correctly, fast, gracefully, hard, kindly, quickly, softly, swiftly, truthfully,* and *well*.

A. Underline the adverb in each sentence that tells *how* or *in what manner*.

1. The court jester danced wildly for the king.

2. The queen wore her crown beautifully.

3. The serfs worked diligently in the fields.

4. They suffered greatly from their poor living conditions.

5. The king spoke distinctly to his subjects.

6. Two guards stood silently at the castle's gate.

7. They proudly protected the castle.

8. The guard carefully aimed his bow and arrow.

9. The king's army fought heroically at the battle.

10. The king and queen danced elegantly at the ball.

B. Complete each sentence with an adverb of manner.

1. Joshua draws and paints _____.

2. He applies the paint _____.

3. His hand draws _____ on the paper.

4. No one speaks _____ in his studio.

5. I go to see his art _____.

6. When I paint, I move the brush _____.

7. I must go to art class _____.

8. In class we paint and draw _____.

9. Josh likes to draw when music is playing _____.

10. He paints _____ every morning.

76. Adverbs of Time, Place, and Manner

Underline the adverb in each sentence.
Write on the line to tell if it expresses time, place, or manner.

_____ 1. In Omaha, Nebraska, Father Edward J. Flanagan regularly studied the plight of young boys who were orphans, delinquents, or criminals.

_____ 2. He decided to work daily for their cause.

_____ 3. For the boys to move successfully through life, they needed an education.

_____ 4. Father Flanagan started what is now the Girls and Boys Town school system.

_____ 5. He earnestly collected money to rent an old mansion as a home for boys.

_____ 6. Father Flanagan's policy was to welcome any boy who wanted to be there.

_____ 7. The boys played sports and frequently played music.

_____ 8. When the school outgrew that space, Father Flanagan determinedly found another.

_____ 9. Father Flanagan bought a farm that was located nearby.

_____ 10. A home could finally be built to accommodate all the boys.

_____ 11. On it the boys could work hard and produce some of their own food.

_____ 12. This home would soon be called Boys Town.

_____ 13. Girls and Boys Towns can be found elsewhere in our country.

_____ 14. Their workers tirelessly serve not only girls and boys but families as well.

_____ 15. We need people like Father Flanagan, who have faith in humanity and who give generously of themselves.

Father Flanagan cared for boys who were outcasts of society. He believed in them when no one else did. Give an example of something kind you can do for someone in your class or school who is not accepted by the crowd.

77. Adverbs That Compare

Many adverbs have three **degrees of comparison: positive, comparative,** and **superlative.**
The comparative of most adverbs that end in *-ly* is formed by adding *more* or *less* before the positive.
The superlative is formed by adding *most* or *least* before the positive.

quickly	more quickly	most quickly
sadly	less sadly	least sadly

The comparative of most adverbs that do not end in *-ly* is formed by adding *-er.* The superlative is formed by adding *-est.*

soon	sooner	soonest
far	farther	farthest

Adverbs

A. Underline the adverb in each sentence.
Write on the line the degree of comparison.

_____ 1. The rooster woke us early in the morning.

_____ 2. A cheetah can run faster than a lion.

_____ 3. The brown puppy opened its eyes widest of all.

_____ 4. In the city you will see squirrels more often than rabbits.

_____ 5. The old man treats his cats kindly.

_____ 6. The crew worked hard at building the dam.

_____ 7. The seagull flew higher than the pelican.

_____ 8. The bear cub tried earnestly to catch a salmon.

_____ 9. A snail travels more slowly than many other animals.

_____ 10. I think the gazelle runs most gracefully of all.

B. Circle the correct adverb in parentheses.

1. Of all the rainy days, today it is raining (harder hardest).

2. You must walk (carefully more carefully) when it is raining than when it is not.

3. We (politely more politely) folded our umbrellas when we entered her house.

4. The eagle flew (high higher) than usual to avoid the rain.

5. This is the (more awful most awful) weather we've had in a long time.

Name _____

78. Good and Well

> The word *good* is an adjective. Adjectives modify nouns or pronouns. *Good* may follow a linking verb as a subject complement.
>
> **The mushroom pizza was a <u>good</u> choice.** (modifies the noun *choice*)
> **They are <u>good</u> at playing soccer.** (modifies the pronoun *they*)
>
> *Good* answers the question *what kind.*
>
> **She was a <u>good</u> babysitter.**
> (*What kind* of babysitter was she? She was a *good* one.)
>
> The word *well* is generally an adverb. Adverbs usually modify verbs. *Well* often modifies a verb and answers the question *how.*
>
> **Susan plays <u>well</u> with other children.**
> (*How* does she play with other children? She plays *well.*)

A. Circle the correct word in parentheses.

1. Andy cleaned his room (good well).

2. This room could use a (good well) dusting.

3. (Good Well) cleaning supplies will help a lot.

4. If we don't dry the window (good well), it will have streaks.

5. Lots of (good well) effort is what we need.

6. Did you know that newspaper dries a mirror or window (good well)?

7. It's a (good well) idea to begin dusting at the top of the walls and work toward the floor.

8. If we don't do a (good well) job, your mother will notice.

9. He doesn't do as (good well) with the broom and the mop as he does with the vacuum cleaner.

10. We have worked together (good well) and now have an immaculate house.

B. Complete each sentence with *good* or *well.*

1. The shining sun seemed to say it was going to be a _____ day.

2. For some reason I couldn't listen _____ in class today.

3. I had no _____ reason for misspelling that easy word.

4. The teacher explained the decimal problem _____.

5. When things don't go _____, I consult my older brother.

Adverbs

82

Name _____

79. Real and Very

> *Real* is an adjective and means "genuine or true."
>
> **Believe it or not, that was a <u>real</u> monkey in our yard.**
>
> *Very* is an adverb and means "extremely or to a high degree."
>
> **Marina was <u>very</u> cautious as she walked along the ledge.**

A. Complete each sentence with *real* or *very*.

1. I am always _____ happy to visit the art museum.

2. You can see many _____ masterpieces there.

3. The art teachers were _____ eager to see Edgar Degas's work.

4. Degas sculpted human figures _____ well.

5. Degas sometimes used _____ ballerinas as models.

6. He was _____ interested in capturing the mood of dancers backstage.

7. The art student had a _____ interest in art depicting dance.

8. The museum shop has a _____ good collection of Degas prints.

9. An art collector would rather have the _____ thing.

10. It was _____ thoughtful of you to buy me this Degas print.

B. Circle the correct word in parentheses.

1. Brioche is a (real very) tasty kind of bread.

2. It is made with lots of (real very) butter.

3. The (real very) recipe calls for a special pan.

4. When I am (real very) hungry, a brioche and some tea are the perfect snack.

5. I am (real very) picky about the breads I eat.

6. They must be (real very) fresh.

7. Fresh bread is a gift of (real very) appeal for many people.

8. The crust is often (real very) brown and crunchy.

9. The (real very) test of whether a bread is good is if Grandma will eat it.

10. Thick slices of fresh bread help make a (real very) hearty sandwich.

80. No, Not, Never

A negative idea is expressed by using one negative word.
This negative word may be *no, not, none, never,* or *nothing.*

There was <u>nothing</u> she could say to make me change my mind.

If a sentence has one negative word, do not add another. Use a word
such as *any* or *ever* instead.

A. Circle the correct word in parentheses.

1. None of my friends has (ever never) seen a farm.

2. Aren't there (any no) farms near the city?

3. I have (ever never) ridden on a tractor.

4. There were (any no) scarecrows in the fields.

5. Didn't she gather (any no) eggs from the hens?

6. Isn't there (anything nothing) I can do for the harvest?

7. Haven't you baled (any no) hay?

8. There are (any no) farmhands on this farm at all.

9. There was (any no) way to save the crop.

10. She has (ever never) seen cattle.

B. Complete each sentence to express a negative idea.

1. Bill hasn't found _____ mail in his mailbox.

2. Have you _____ received a package by special delivery?

3. I have _____ been sent flowers.

4. Did you _____ bring stamps with you?

5. This package hasn't _____ postage.

6. There was _____ address on this envelope.

7. Vince has _____ had a pen pal.

8. You can't write if you haven't _____ stationery.

9. Haven't you _____ received a chain letter?

10. Aren't there _____ mailboxes nearby?

Name _____

81. There Is and There Are

When a sentence begins with *there* followed by a form of the verb *be,* the subject of the sentence comes after the verb. *There is* or *there was* is used with a singular subject. *There are* or *there were* is used with a plural subject.

	VERB		SUBJECT	
There	is	a large	tree	in our backyard.
There	are		flowers	growing under the tree.

A. Underline the subject of each sentence. Write **S** if the subject is singular or **P** if the subject is plural.

_____ 1. There are several parks in downtown Chicago.

_____ 2. There are modern sculptures in Millennium Park.

_____ 3. There is a sculpture that looks like a huge, shiny bean.

_____ 4. There is a large fountain with two tall towers.

_____ 5. There are pictures of faces projected on the towers.

_____ 6. There is shallow water for children to play in.

_____ 7. There is a stage in the park.

_____ 8. There are concerts there in the summertime.

_____ 9. There are restaurants near the stage.

_____ 10. There are many things to do and see.

B. Write *was* or *were* to complete each sentence.

1. There _____ a kite festival in my neighborhood last week.

2. There _____ kites of every size and shape.

3. There _____ free kite-making kits for children.

4. There _____ an instructor who taught us how to fly kites.

5. There _____ strolling musicians.

6. There _____ a food cart at the edge of the field.

7. There _____ a craft booth where kids made kite-shaped magnets.

8. There _____ clowns walking on stilts.

9. There _____ a nice breeze that day.

10. There _____ dozens of kites in the sky.

Adverbs

82. Adverb Clauses

A **clause** is a group of words with a subject and a predicate. An **independent clause** expresses a complete thought and can stand on its own as a sentence. A **dependent clause** does not express a complete thought and cannot stand on its own as a sentence. An **adverb clause** is a dependent clause used as an adverb. An adverb clause often answers the question *when*. Common conjunctions used to introduce adverb clauses are *after, as, as soon as, before, once, since, until, when, whenever,* and *while*.

> I will do my homework <u>before we eat dinner</u>.
> <u>After I do the dishes</u>, I'll play video games.

Underline the adverb clause in each sentence. Look for the conjunctions for help.

1. Kit Carson's father died when Kit was only nine years old.

2. After Kit turned fourteen, he became a saddle maker.

3. When Kit was nineteen, he moved west and became a fur trapper.

4. While he was trapping, he got to know many Native Americans.

5. Whenever people talked about Kit, they said he was brave and honest.

6. Kit met John Frémont while Kit was visiting Missouri.

7. Kit guided John as they traveled all over the West.

8. When John published his journal of the trip, Kit became famous.

9. Kit led U.S. troops when war broke out with Mexico in 1846.

10. After the war ended, Kit became a rancher in the New Mexico Territory.

11. He served as a federal Indian agent for northern New Mexico until the Civil War started.

12. When the Civil War broke out, Kit helped organize New Mexico's infantry.

13. Before Kit retired, he moved Navajos from their land to a reservation.

14. As soon as the war was over, Kit left the army and went back to ranching.

15. Since his death in 1868, there have been books, movies, and television shows about his life.

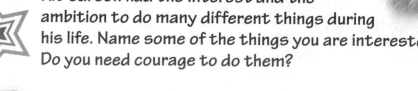

Kit Carson had the interest and the ambition to do many different things during his life. Name some of the things you are interested in doing. Do you need courage to do them?

Adverbs

83. Reviewing Adverbs

A. Write on the line whether the *italicized* adverb is an adverb of time, place, or manner.

_____ 1. A storm hit our town *yesterday*.

_____ 2. The sky *quickly* got dark.

_____ 3. *Next* the wind began to gust.

_____ 4. Thunder cracked *overhead*.

_____ 5. Rain beat *loudly* against the windows.

B. Complete the chart with the comparative and superlative of each adverb.

	COMPARATIVE	SUPERLATIVE
6. fast	_____	_____
7. faithfully	_____	_____
8. swiftly	_____	_____
9. high	_____	_____
10. far	_____	_____

C. Write *is* or *are* to complete each sentence.

11. There _____ a great park near my house.

12. There _____ swings and slides for little kids.

13. There _____ softball fields too.

14. There _____ a pool for swimmers.

15. There _____ activities for everyone.

D. Underline the adverb clause in each sentence. Look for the conjunctions for help.

16. Before we leave for the lake, we pack up the car.

17. We sing silly songs while we are on the way.

18. As soon as we arrive, we run for the water.

19. When we are tired of swimming, we eat lunch.

20. We hike in the woods after we take a nap.

Adverbs

CONTINUED

E. **Circle the correct word in parentheses.**

21. The poor man went to Abinuku for (well good) advice.

22. Abinuku was (very real) jealous of him.

23. Abinuku (ever never) wanted the poor man to be happy.

24. "You must choose (good well)," Abinuku said.

25. "(None No) other decision should be considered as carefully as this one."

26. "A (good well) choice," he said, "would be Patience."

27. Abinuku thought, "It won't bring him (no any) happiness."

28. The poor man wanted (nothing anything) but to make the right choice.

29. At first his wife was (very real) angry.

30. Eventually, however, Patience brought them (very real) joy.

31. (Nothing None) of the other gifts could have made them more content.

32. They couldn't remember (ever never) being so happy.

33. Money and Child came to the couple too, and they were (ever never) a problem.

34. The couple didn't need (no any) other gifts.

35. In the end Abinuku had advised the poor man (good well).

Adverbs

Try It Yourself
**Write four sentences about a storm or other severe weather
you have witnessed. Be sure to use adverbs correctly.**

_____

_____

_____

_____

Check Your Own Work
**Choose a selection from your writing portfolio, your journal,
a work in progress, an assignment from another class, or a letter.
Revise it, applying the skills you have reviewed.
This checklist will help you.**

✔ Have you included appropriate adverbs of time, place, and manner?

✔ Have you used the correct degree of comparison for the adverbs?

✔ Have you used *good* and *well*, negative words, and *real* and *very* correctly?

84. Prepositions and Their Objects

> A **preposition** is a word that shows the relationship between a noun or a pronoun and another word in the sentence. The noun or pronoun that follows the preposition is the **object of the preposition.**
>
> **Little Red Riding Hood went <u>into</u> the woods.**
> (*Woods* is the object of the preposition *into.*)
>
> Here are some common prepositions.
>
> | | | | | | |
> |---|---|---|---|---|---|
> | about | against | between | for | of | to |
> | above | among | by | from | off | toward |
> | across | at | down | in | on | under |
> | after | before | during | into | over | up |
> | around | beside | except | near | through | with |

A. Complete each sentence with an appropriate preposition.

1. We enjoyed sledding _____ the hill.

2. James slid _____ a snow bank.

3. Don't fall _____ the sled, Luchi.

4. Vince took the ski lift _____ the mountain.

5. He skied _____ the slopes.

6. We took a sleigh ride _____ the woods.

7. The ride took us _____ a stream.

8. We went _____ a snow-covered bridge.

9. Ice skate _____ us, Anna.

10. Her skates were a gift _____ her aunt.

B. Circle the prepositions in these sentences.

1. John Chapman was born in Massachusetts in 1775.

2. Johnny's dream was planting apple trees for settlers.

3. His dream could not come true without hard work.

4. He went into several orchards and collected a lot of seeds.

5. A law required that settlers plant 50 trees on their land.

85. Prepositional Phrases

A preposition and the noun or pronoun that follows it are separate words, but they do the work of a single modifier. This group of related words is called a phrase. Because it is introduced by a preposition, it is called a **prepositional phrase**.

Little Red Riding Hood went <u>into the woods</u>.

A. Circle the preposition(s) and underline the prepositional phrase(s) in each sentence.

1. At first John Chapman gave bags of seeds to settlers.

2. Later he traveled to Pennsylvania.

3. After some time, he journeyed to the Ohio Valley.

4. Johnny took saplings with him everywhere.

5. He planted them beside running streams.

6. He also planted orchards on rolling hills.

7. He could not notice a fertile area without stopping.

8. Johnny moved from place to place, planting more trees.

9. Throughout the area he became known as Johnny Appleseed.

10. Thanks to him, the Ohio Valley is rich in apple trees.

B. Complete each sentence with a prepositional phrase.

1. The gardener bent _____.

2. He planted the wildflower seeds _____.

3. He put some ladybugs _____.

4. I gave the gardener a spade, which he placed _____.

5. The gardener placed a bouquet _____.

90

Prepositions, Conjunctions, Interjections

86. Between and Among

Use the preposition *between* when speaking of two persons, places, or things.
   Let's keep this information between you and me.

Use the preposition *among* when speaking of more than two persons, places, or things.
   The singer stood unrecognized among her fans.

A. Circle the correct preposition in parentheses.

1. Amy walked (between among) her two sisters.
2. The United States lies (between among) the Atlantic and the Pacific oceans.
3. Distribute the papers (between among) the students in the class.
4. A beautiful flower grew (between among) the dozens of weeds.
5. The band marched (between among) two lines of spectators.
6. The two boys carried the injured man (between among) them.
7. Four of the Great Lakes lie (between among) the United States and Canada.
8. Is there a secret (between among) the two of you?
9. Our airplane is (between among) those three on the runway.
10. You may sit (between among) Austin and me.
11. Alabama is (between among) Georgia and Mississippi.
12. Good leaders work for peace (between among) all the nations of the world.
13. Share the fruit (between among) the four of you.
14. The flower arrangement sat (between among) two candles.
15. Not one (between among) the students would miss the field trip.

B. Complete each sentence with *between* or *among*.

1. Those five boys often quarrel _____ themselves.
2. Trade is carried on _____ North and South America.
3. There isn't one tall player _____ the five.
4. _____ you and me, whom shall we choose?
5. The awards were divided _____ the three top winners.
6. There is a joyful spirit _____ the students in our class.
7. The garage stands _____ the house and the barn.
8. There was one stranger _____ the four visitors.
9. _____ them, the two brothers made the model ship.
10. May I walk _____ Ian and you?

Name _____

87. From and Off

From generally refers to moving away; it indicates a starting point for a physical movement. *From* may also refer to the source of something.

> **We traveled from Virginia to New Jersey.**
> **The invitation was from my neighbors.**

Off is used to indicate the removal or separation of something. The expression *off of* is never correct.

> CORRECT: **He took the tag off his shirt.**
> INCORRECT: **He took the tag off of his shirt.**

A. Circle the correct preposition in parentheses.

1. The label came (from off) the jar when it got wet.

2. We bought corn (from off) the farmer.

3. She swept the leaves (off of off) the porch.

4. (From Off) whom did you receive that interesting book?

5. Take the message (from off) him, please.

6. Who slid (off of off) the seat?

7. These skates are a gift (from off) my uncle.

8. The boy hopped (from off) his bicycle.

9. This watch is a present (from off) my grandparents.

10. It was hard to get the top (off of off) the ketchup bottle.

B. Complete each sentence with *from* or *off*.

1. Don't jump _____ the step.

2. We get peanuts _____ farmers.

3. The farmhand hopped _____ the tractor.

4. My mother buys spices _____ that shopkeeper.

5. I get interesting books _____ my uncle.

6. The sign read, "Keep _____ the grass."

7. The lid fell _____ the jar.

8. Kevin stepped _____ the train quickly.

9. I learned how to print _____ my teacher.

10. You may get a paper _____ the instructor.

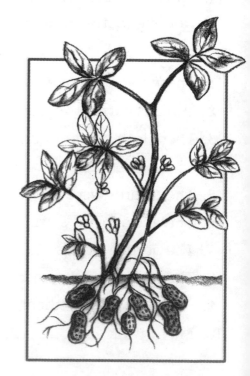

88. Prepositional Phrases as Adjectives

> An **adjective phrase** is a prepositional phrase used as an adjective.
> An adjective phrase contains a preposition and an object.
> **The ballerina <u>with the pink tutu</u> danced gracefully.**

A. Underline the adjective phrase in each sentence. Identify the noun each adjective phrase modifies. Write the noun on the line.

_____ 1. The flowers in the vase look lovely.

_____ 2. They are from the garden behind the house.

_____ 3. The roses along the trellis are red, yellow, and pink.

_____ 4. The ivy on the house is growing quickly.

_____ 5. The tree beside the house shades the lawn.

_____ 6. The daffodils with yellow trumpets stand nearby.

_____ 7. The zinnias near the trellis are very cheerful.

_____ 8. The shrub in the corner is fragrant and colorful.

_____ 9. The lilies in this garden have showy flowers.

_____ 10. The plant with heart-shaped flowers is called a bleeding heart.

B. Read the paragraph. Underline the adjective phrases. Circle the noun each phrase modifies.

Are you a person with hay fever? Hay fever is an allergy with definite symptoms. All seasons except winter are bad times for sufferers. This allergy produces uncomfortable irritations in the eyes, nose, and throat. The eyes of the victim may become red, itchy, and watery. The nose with its swollen membranes may itch and run. The throat with its sensitivity becomes irritated. What is the cause of all this grief? Pollen from plants is the culprit! If you have symptoms of this annoying condition, many remedies are available.

89. More Prepositional Phrases as Adjectives

Rewrite each sentence, changing the *italicized* adjective
to an adjective phrase.

1. The *tour* guide spoke perfect English.

   _____

2. She pointed out the *marble* statue.

   _____

3. Then she showed us the *Vermeer* painting.

   _____

4. The *gold* crown was behind glass.

   _____

5. We could touch the *silver* rings though.

   _____

6. A *German* tourist asked many questions.

   _____

7. His friends wanted to stop for some *Italian* coffee.

   _____

8. We were all hoping there would be some *French* bread.

   _____

9. We settled for *cheese* sandwiches.

   _____

10. The *tour* bus could not fit between the cars.

    _____

    _____

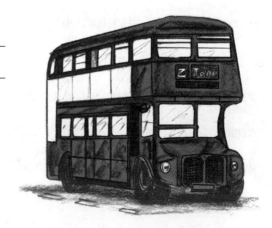

Name _____

90. Prepositional Phrases as Adverbs

> An **adverb phrase** is a prepositional phrase used as an adverb.
> An adverb phrase contains a preposition and an object.
>
> **The rain drove the team <u>into the dugout</u>.**

A. Underline the adverb phrase in each sentence.
Write on the line the verb it modifies.

_____ 1. The tour guide's words led us into the past.

_____ 2. She described the knights who jousted outside the castle walls.

_____ 3. The lord of the castle watched from the battlements.

_____ 4. His lady sat in the tower.

_____ 5. The guards lowered the drawbridge over the moat.

_____ 6. When drawn, the bridge stood against the gate.

_____ 7. The guards shot arrows through the loopholes in the castle walls.

_____ 8. All the castle's residents feasted in the great hall.

_____ 9. The lady disappeared up the spiral staircase.

_____ 10. The feast's herbs and vegetables came from the castle's small garden.

B. Complete each sentence with an adverb phrase.

1. The plane flies _____

2. We traveled _____

3. We gave our passports _____

4. The guide placed our bags _____

5. The pickpocket reached _____

6. We bought the strange fruit _____

7. I put the train tickets _____

8. My passport fell _____

9. We misplaced the money _____

10. We won't travel again _____

91. More Prepositional Phrases as Adverbs

Rewrite each sentence, changing the *italicized* adverb
to an adverb phrase.

1. The surgeon operated *skillfully* on the patient.

   _____

2. The patient lay *silently* on the operating table.

   _____

3. Her husband paced *worriedly* up and down the hallway.

   _____

4. The patient recovered *speedily*.

   _____

5. The bandages were changed *gently* by the nurse.

   _____

6. The night nurse ran the unit *efficiently*.

   _____

7. The technician performed the tests *quickly*.

   _____

8. The elderly patient moved her leg *painfully*.

   _____

9. The orderly pushed the gurney *clumsily* into the elevator.

   _____

10. The doctor diagnosed the problem *expertly*.

   _____

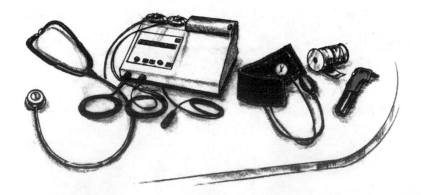

Name _____

92. Prepositional Phrases as Adjectives or Adverbs

Read the sentences. Circle the adjective phrases. Underline the adverb phrases.

1. The Statue of Liberty stands in New York Harbor.

2. It was erected in 1886.

3. It was a gift from France.

4. *Liberty Enlightening the World* was the name the artist gave to the statue.

5. "The New Colossus" was another name given to the statue.

6. This title comes from a poem.

7. The poem was written by Emma Lazarus.

8. She was a poet from New York City.

9. She called the statue "Mother of Exiles" in her poem.

10. The statue in the poem gives a "world-wide welcome."

11. What she wrote in her poem was heartfelt.

12. In the late 1800s America was welcoming numerous immigrants.

13. These were immigrants from many nations.

14. Emma cared particularly about the Jewish people who came here, because she herself was Jewish.

15. Her family could trace its Jewish heritage to America's early settlement.

16. Emma spoke on Jewish issues.

17. She started classes for Jewish immigrants.

18. She helped them find housing in the city.

19. She published her poem "The New Colossus" in 1883.

20. Her poem eventually was engraved on the Statue of Liberty's plaque.

Emma Lazarus tried to help people who were new to this country. Give an example of something you can do to help someone who is new to your class, school, or neighborhood.

93. Conjunctions with Subjects

> A **conjunction** is a word that connects words or groups of words.
>
> **Would you like to play volleyball or soccer?**
>
> The most common conjunctions are coordinating conjunctions such as *and, or,* and *but.* A **coordinating conjunction** connects words or groups of words that are of equal importance in a sentence, such as the parts of a compound subject. A sentence with two or more subjects has a **compound subject.**
>
> **Women and men sprinted after the dog.**

A. **Circle the conjunction in each sentence. Underline the subjects it connects.**

1. Today and tomorrow will be special program days at my school.
2. The students or the teachers are going to sit in the front rows in the gym.
3. Tracy and Trina will sit next to each other on the bleachers.
4. The cheerleaders or the basketball players will act as ushers.
5. Singing and dancing will be the main events.
6. The band and the bandleader have practiced.
7. A singer or a dancer will be the featured attraction.
8. Talk and laughter will fill the gym.
9. The lead singer and the chorus sing soulfully.
10. The music and dance mesmerize the audience.

B. **Complete each sentence with a coordinating conjunction to connect the subjects.**

1. Elizabeth _____ Tina study together.
2. He _____ I will borrow the class notes.
3. The teacher _____ the aide will administer the test.
4. Not you _____ I am unprepared for this test.
5. The test _____ an answer grid were placed on my desk.

C. **Complete each sentence with a compound subject.**

1. _____ and _____ like picnics.
2. _____ and _____ were placed on the ground.
3. Not _____ but _____ brought the grill.
4. I'd like _____ or _____ to drink but not both.
5. _____ but not _____ goes on all afternoon.

94. Conjunctions with Predicates

> Two or more predicates joined by a coordinating conjunction form a **compound predicate**.
>
> **The picnickers talked and ate all afternoon.**

A. **Circle the conjunction in each sentence.
Underline the verbs it connects.**

1. I awake and slide out of bed.

2. I wash and dry my face.

3. For breakfast I toast some bread
   or fix cereal with fruit.

4. I put on my hat and pull on my gloves.

5. I take my backpack but often carry my lunch.

6. I wave and yell to get the bus driver's attention.

7. My friends talk or sing on the bus.

8. We are tested and quizzed on many subjects.

9. I usually walk but sometimes run to the bus stop.

10. The teacher listens and comments thoughtfully each time I talk.

B. **Complete each sentence. Use a conjunction to connect the verbs.**

1. The baby cried _____ laughed at different times today.

2. The mother hugged _____ kissed the baby.

3. The father did not feed _____ washed the baby.

4. The baby cannot walk _____ talk yet.

5. The baby's cereal heats _____ bubbles quickly.

C. **Complete each sentence with a compound predicate.**

1. The old car _____ and _____ .

2. We _____ and _____ it.

3. Afterward it _____ and _____ in the sun.

4. We _____ and _____ to our friends as we
   drove it through town.

5. It _____ and _____ when we changed gears.

95. Conjunctions with Direct Objects

> A verb that has two or more direct objects has a **compound direct object.** The parts of a compound direct object are connected by a coordinating conjunction.
>
> **The carpenter carried a <u>hammer</u> <u>and</u> <u>a saw.</u>**

A. **Circle the conjunction in each sentence. Underline the direct objects it connects.**

1. Airplanes transport mail and passengers.

2. Many passengers like takeoff but not landing.

3. Flight attendants offer food and drinks to passengers.

4. Meals usually include beef or chicken.

5. Passengers often have cell phones and laptop computers.

6. Flight attendants explain safety precautions and flight rules.

7. They also mention seat belts and floatation devices.

8. Often a flight attendant must practice patience and kindness with a troublesome passenger.

9. The pilot announces the plane's current location and its estimated time of arrival.

10. Flight attendants provide not entertainment but safety.

B. **Complete each sentence. Use a conjunction to connect the direct objects.**

1. The model was wearing a blue coat _____ a hat.

2. She applied powder _____ blush to her face.

3. Her agent didn't like her makeup _____ her clothes.

4. The photographer scrutinized the shadows _____ light on the model's face.

5. The model offered not frowns _____ smiles to the camera.

C. **Complete each sentence with a compound direct object.**

1. For a first course we're offered _____ but not _____.

2. The waiter will serve _____ and _____ for dessert.

3. We left our _____ and _____ at the coat check.

4. We could take a _____ or a _____ home.

5. We could watch _____ or a _____ once we got home.

96. Conjunctions with Subject Complements

> A sentence that has two or more subject complements has a **compound subject complement**. The parts of a compound subject complement are connected by a coordinating conjunction.
>
> **Our study of the original colonies was <u>interesting</u> and <u>enlightening</u>.**

A. Circle the coordinating conjunction in each sentence. Underline the subject complements it connects.

1. Many of the original colonists were farmers or trappers.

2. The soil in New England was thin and rocky.

3. Winters were very cold and snowy.

4. Some of New England's primary goods were lumber and fish.

5. Its manufactured products were ships and clothing.

6. The main foods raised in the Middle Colonies were vegetables and grain.

7. The soil in these colonies was rich and fertile.

8. Summer in the Southern Colonies was hot and humid.

9. The main crops grown in the Southern Colonies were rice and tobacco.

10. Some of the native people were the Algonquin and the Wampanoag.

B. Complete each sentence with a conjunction to connect the subject complements.

1. The founders of most of the colonies were English _____ Dutch.

2. The settlers were brave _____ energetic.

3. Their main needs were food _____ tools.

4. The things they desired were land _____ freedom.

5. The native people they met could be friends _____ enemies.

C. Complete each sentence with a compound subject complement.

1. My favorite subjects are _____ and _____.

2. I like them because they are _____ and _____.

3. My best friends are _____ and _____.

4. My friends like me because I am _____ and _____.

5. My favorite hobbies are _____ and _____.

Prepositions, Conjunctions, Interjections

101

97. Conjunctions with Sentences

> Sentences can be connected by a conjunction. Two complete sentences joined by a coordinating conjunction form a **compound sentence**.
>
> **I kept the sturdy raincoat, <u>but</u> I returned the flimsy jacket.**

A. Read the two sentences in each example. Add a conjunction to connect the two sentences. Use *and, but,* or *or.* In some cases, more than one conjunction may be correct.

1. Diamonds are precious gems, _____ they are also used for industry.

2. You can wear diamonds on your fingers, _____ you can use diamonds to cut glass.

3. The diamond was insured, _____ she was still afraid to wear it.

4. You must clean and polish your diamond ring, _____ it will look dull.

5. A cubic zirconia may look like a diamond, _____ it doesn't cost as much.

6. The diamond is not my birthstone, _____ I want one anyway.

7. Her diamond was square, _____ it had sapphires on its sides.

8. She might give the diamond ring to her daughter, _____ she might donate it to charity.

9. The diamond shimmered, _____ its gold setting shone.

10. She wore no diamonds or gold, _____ she looked like a princess anyway.

B. Circle the conjunction in each sentence. Underline the words the conjunction connects. Write on the line whether the conjunction connects subjects, verbs, direct objects, subject complements, or sentences.

_____ 1. Our class art project on color required paint and water.

_____ 2. First we filled jars and glasses with water.

_____ 3. Next we gathered paints and brushes together.

_____ 4. Paper and charts were hung around the room.

_____ 5. Then the boys and the girls had a contest.

_____ 6. Trudy mixed blue and yellow to make green.

_____ 7. The colors Ted used were red and blue.

_____ 8. He mixed and blended the colors to get violet.

_____ 9. Tara mixed red and green together.

_____ 10. It didn't look like a color, but it did look like mud!

Name _____

98. Subordinate Conjunctions

A clause has a subject and a predicate. An independent clause expresses a complete thought and can stand alone as a sentence. A dependent clause does not express a complete thought and cannot stand alone as a sentence. A **subordinate conjunction** introduces a dependent clause and connects it to the independent clause. Many subordinate conjunctions tell *when*. They include *after, as, as soon as, before, once, since, when, whenever, while,* and *until.*

> **After** the Civil War ended, African Americans looked for business opportunities.
> Many women worked as maids <u>until</u> they could find better jobs.

Circle the subordinate conjunction in each sentence.

1. Sarah Breedlove was orphaned when she was seven years old.

2. She married and had a daughter while she was just a teenager.

3. After her husband died, Sarah moved to St. Louis.

4. She worked as a washerwoman until a scalp ailment made her hair fall out.

5. After trying several hair treatments, she realized that there were few hair products especially for African American women.

6. When she tried products made by another black woman, her scalp condition improved.

7. As soon as she could, she started selling hair products to black women.

8. After Sarah moved to Denver in 1905, she married C. J. Walker.

9. Once they became business partners, she changed her name to Madame C. J. Walker.

10. After creating her own line of products, Walker began selling them door-to-door.

11. As the business grew, Madame Walker hired other women to sell her products.

12. She continued to work hard until she had more than 3,000 employees.

13. After years of struggling, Madame Walker became America's first self-made female millionaire.

14. Whenever she found a good cause, she donated money to it.

15. Since her death in 1919, she has been regarded as a role model by many women.

 Madame C. J. Walker worked hard to become a successful businessperson. Give an example of how you can work hard to be successful at something.

99. Interjections

> An **interjection** expresses a strong feeling or emotion. Listed below are some common interjections and the emotions they could express.
>
> | | | | |
> |---|---|---|---|
> | JOY | **Hurrah! Bravo! Great! Oh!** | WONDER | **Ah! Oh!** |
> | DISGUST | **Oh! Ick! Yuck! Ugh!** | SORROW | **Oh! Ah!** |
> | CAUTION | **Hush! Shh! Uh-oh!** | IMPATIENCE | **Goodness! Well!** |
> | PAIN | **Oh! Ouch!** | SURPRISE | **What! Oh! Aha! Wow!** |

A. Underline the interjections. Write on the line what emotion each interjection expresses.

_____ 1. Great! You're here.

_____ 2. Well! We should be in our seats by now.

_____ 3. Oh! This opera house is magnificent.

_____ 4. Ouch! This seat isn't comfortable.

_____ 5. Uh-oh! The first act is about to begin.

_____ 6. Oh! The story is terribly sad.

_____ 7. Ah! Her voice is really beautiful.

_____ 8. What! It's almost over.

_____ 9. Shh! They're still singing.

_____ 10. They sang so well. Bravo!

B. Write appropriate interjections on the lines.

_____ 1. Move out of the way of the bus.

_____ 2. It splashed me with that mucky water.

_____ 3. My coat is ruined.

_____ 4. You have a clean one I can borrow?

_____ 5. Now we can still go out.

_____ 6. I don't think I can go.

_____ 7. Is something the matter?

_____ 8. I have a terrible headache.

_____ 9. I thought you weren't acting like your usual cheerful self.

_____ 10. We'll miss you if you go home.

Name _____

100. Reviewing Prepositions, Conjunctions, and Interjections

A. Circle the preposition in each sentence.
Underline the prepositional phrase.

1. The lawyer walked toward the courthouse.

2. The papers in his briefcase were exhibits.

3. He got home quite late every night during the trial.

4. The judge sat inside his chambers.

5. They put the defendant on the stand.

B. Circle the correct preposition in parentheses.

6. The shirts were distributed (between among) the members of the team.

7. Just (between among) you and me, I don't like them.

8. Their color is somewhere (between among) green and yellow.

9. We bought them (from off) a dealer for a reduced price.

10. I'll never take it (from off) if we win a game.

C. Write on the lines below whether each *italicized* phrase
is used as an adjective or an adverb.

The tree *on the hill* was struck *by lightning*. The mishap occurred
        11.   **12.**
during a violent storm. It was a hot day *in August*. The dark clouds rolled
    13.   **14.**
across the sky. Raindrops *of enormous size* pelted the countryside. Thunder
  15.   **16.**
echoed *with loud booms*, and lightning darted *across the heavens*. It lasted
    17.   **18.**
for a short time only. Then the dark clouds were replaced *by blue sky*.
    19.   **20.**

11. _____   16. _____

12. _____   17. _____

13. _____   18. _____

14. _____   19. _____

15. _____   20. _____

D. Write on the line whether the *italicized* conjunction connects subjects, verbs, direct objects, subject complements, or sentences.

_____ 21. Mike Fink *and* Paul Bunyan are folk heroes.

_____ 22. People tell *and* retell stories about them.

_____ 23. They performed amazing feats *and* heroic deeds.

_____ 24. Mike had a great appetite, *but* Paul could eat more.

_____ 25. For breakfast Paul ate 100 pancakes *and* drank 14 gallons of milk.

_____ 26. Paul farmed the Rocky Mountain Valley *and* the Colorado River Valley.

_____ 27. He used Babe the Blue Ox *and* a huge plow.

_____ 28. Mike *or* Paul would have helped anyone.

_____ 29. They were strong *but* kind.

_____ 30. Both have died, *but* their memories live on.

E. Write appropriate interjections on the lines.

_____ 31. Mike Fink is aiming for the mosquito on the fence.

_____ 32. Did Mike jump across the Ohio River?

_____ 33. Those two were amazing.

_____ 34. She's telling the story of another folk hero.

_____ 35. I love these stories.

Try It Yourself.

Write three sentences about your favorite folktale character. Use prepositional phrases, conjunctions, and at least one interjection in your sentences.

_____

_____

_____

Check Your Own Work

Choose a selection from your writing portfolio, your journal, a work in progress, an assignment from another class, or a letter. Revise it, applying the skills you have reviewed. This checklist will help you.

✔ Have you used appropriate prepositions?

✔ Have you used *between*, *among*, *from*, and *off* correctly?

✔ Have you used interjections that express the correct emotions?

Name _____

101. Complete Sentences

A **sentence** is a group of words that expresses a complete thought.
Every sentence has a subject and a predicate.

SUBJECT | PREDICATE

That busy lawyer **devotes some of her time to charity work.**

A. Read each example. Write **S** on the line if the words form a sentence.
Write **NS** on the line if the words do not form a sentence.

_____ 1. Many years ago.

_____ 2. Most pioneers traveled in covered wagons.

_____ 3. Sometimes large families and even a dog.

_____ 4. Early in the morning.

_____ 5. They made bread in cast iron pans.

_____ 6. Often slept under their wagons.

_____ 7. Some of the wagons were pulled by oxen.

_____ 8. Met Indians on the plains.

_____ 9. Became sick on their journey.

_____ 10. No doctor to help them.

_____ 11. The dangerous snow-covered mountains.

_____ 12. The deserts were very hard on the animals.

_____ 13. Occasionally the pioneers became lost.

_____ 14. Many of the pioneers were immigrants.

_____ 15. Founded new towns out west.

B. Write a complete sentence, using each group of words.
Be sure to start each sentence with a capital letter and
end it with the correct punctuation mark.

when it rains   1. _____

alone at night   2. _____

in the attic   3. _____

is scary   4. _____

in the mirror   5. _____

102. Four Kinds of Sentences

There are four kinds of sentences:
declarative, interrogative, imperative, and exclamatory.

A **declarative sentence** makes a statement. It ends with a period.

> **The weather is beautiful today.**

An **interrogative sentence** asks a question. It ends with a question mark.

> **Will I need my umbrella?**

An **imperative sentence** gives a command or makes a request.
It ends with a period. The subject is generally understood to be *you*.

> **Wear this waterproof jacket.**

An **exclamatory sentence** expresses strong emotion.
It ends with an exclamation point.

> **I told you not to go out in the rain!**

**Add the end punctuation to each sentence. Decide if the sentence
is declarative, interrogative, imperative, or exclamatory.
Write your answer on the line.**

_____ 1. Have you ever read Greek mythology

_____ 2. Name some of the ancient gods and goddesses

_____ 3. How fascinating the stories are

_____ 4. My favorite myth is about Medusa

_____ 5. Do you know the god of war

_____ 6. Pegasus is a horse with wings

_____ 7. Name a mythological creature

_____ 8. How mighty Zeus was

_____ 9. Is Venus the goddess of love

_____ 10. What a fearsome creature is the Minotaur

_____ 11. Who was the boy who tried to fly

_____ 12. Hercules was a Greek hero known for his great strength

_____ 13. List Hercules' 12 labors

_____ 14. How angry Hera gets

_____ 15. Did Argus, the hundred-eyed monster, see you

103. Simple Subjects and Simple Predicates

The **subject** names the person, place, or thing that the sentence is about.
The **simple subject** is a pronoun or a noun without any of its modifiers.

> The kind young <u>man</u> helped the elderly woman across the street.

The **predicate** tells what the subject is or does. The **simple predicate** is a verb or a verb phrase without any of its modifiers, objects, or complements.

> The kind young man <u>helped</u> the elderly woman across the street.

Read each sentence. Underline the simple subject and circle the simple predicate.

1. Norman Rockwell is one of the most well-known American artists.

2. He lived first in New York and then in Vermont.

3. He enrolled in art school at the age of 14.

4. The Boy Scouts of America hired him in his late teens as the art director of its publication *Boys' Life*.

5. He painted 321 magazine covers for *The Saturday Evening Post*.

6. Rockwell supported civil rights and the exploration of space.

7. He also cared about poverty in America.

8. Some of his paintings illustrate these things.

9. Most of Rockwell's works depict everyday America.

10. Rockwell's subjects include dogs and children, baseball and barbershops.

Norman Rockwell painted and illustrated everyday America, but he also depicted things that interested or concerned him. He wanted other people to care about these things too. Give an example of how you can share one of your interests or concerns.

104. Complete Subjects

The subject with all its modifiers is called the **complete subject**.

The street artist with his guitar and harmonica entertained the tourists passing by.

A. Read each sentence. Circle the simple subject and underline the complete subject.

1. The Jamestown colonists arrived in America in 1607.

2. The 104 male settlers in Jamestown had many problems.

3. The water near the town was bad for drinking.

4. Many dangerous insects lived around the swampy colony.

5. Insect bites caused disease among the settlers.

6. The men in the colony didn't know how to hunt or fish.

7. The people of Jamestown asked John Smith to be their leader.

8. The resourceful Smith helped the people work together to survive.

9. The grateful colonists began to store food for the winter.

10. Some helpful American Indians taught the colonists to grow corn.

B. Complete each sentence with a descriptive adjective or an adjective phrase. Put parentheses around the complete subjects.

1. The ice _____ has thawed.

2. The ice skates _____ can't be used.

3. The _____ snow has almost disappeared.

4. The trees _____ will soon have tiny buds.

5. The birds _____ will soon fly north.

Sentences

105. Complete Predicates

> The predicate with all its modifiers, objects, and complements is called the **complete predicate**.
>
> **The hungry child <u>ate pizza, pasta, and salad for dinner</u>.**

A. Read each sentence. Circle the simple predicate and underline the complete predicate.

1. Most of the settlers in the New England colonies arrived there from England.

2. They lived in villages like their old ones in England.

3. Many villages had a meeting house in the center.

4. The settlers used the meeting house as a church.

5. They talked about village problems there.

6. The Middle Colonies had good land for farming.

7. The people in these colonies came from many different lands.

8. The colonists did not all practice the same religious faith.

9. Colonists in New York spoke 18 different languages.

10. Colonists in the Middle Colonies sold wheat to people in other colonies.

B. Complete the sentences with modifiers, objects, or complements. Put parentheses around the complete predicates.

1. Thomas was given _____

2. Ken ate _____

3. Catherine wrote _____

4. Lightning streaked _____

5. The tourists crowded _____

6. Mike told _____

7. Weeds grew _____

8. The car stopped _____

9. The terrier bounded _____

10. The pilot climbed _____

106. Direct Objects and Indirect Objects

> The **direct object** is a noun or a pronoun that answers the question *whom* or *what* after an action verb.
>
> **In 1985 three-year-old Lang Lang began playing the <u>piano</u>.**
>
> The **indirect object** tells *to whom, for whom, to what,* or *for what* an action is done. The indirect object comes between the action verb and the direct object.
>
> **Professor Zhu Ya-Fen gave <u>Lang Lang</u> his first piano lessons.**

A. Underline the direct object in each sentence.

1. At age five Lang Lang won first prize in the Shenyang Piano Competition.
2. Soon after that he gave his first piano recital.
3. He won a piano competition in Germany at age 11.
4. At 14 he performed a piece with the China National Symphony.
5. The next year he began his studies in Philadelphia.

B. Circle the indirect object in each sentence. The direct object is underlined.

1. Lang Lang's father taught him traditional Chinese <u>music</u>.
2. Lang Lang gave his father the <u>opportunity</u> to play Chinese music in America.
3. The United Nations offered Lang Lang the <u>position</u> of Goodwill Ambassador.
4. Lang Lang gives children of the world his <u>support</u>.
5. On *Sesame Street* Lang Lang showed Elmo the <u>benefits</u> of exercising to music.

C. Underline the direct object in each sentence. Circle the indirect object.

1. Mrs. Carter teaches students music at Hawthorn School.
2. She assigned Carla a piece by Mozart.
3. Carla gave Mrs. Carter her full attention.
4. Harold showed Paul his new guitar.
5. Paul promised Harold some help after rehearsal.
6. Maria lent Inez a copy of the song.
7. Mrs. Carter bought the class tickets to a concert.
8. She offered them the opportunity to hear professional musicians.
9. The students wrote Mrs. Carter a letter of thanks.
10. They paid her many compliments.

107. Subject Complements

A **subject complement** completes the meaning of a linking verb. It is part of the predicate. If the subject complement is a noun, it renames the subject. If the subject complement is an adjective, it describes the subject.

Anne Sullivan was an orphan.
She was almost blind.

A. **Circle the subject complement in each sentence. Write N if it is a noun or A if it is an adjective.**

_____ 1. Anne Sullivan was the best student in her class at the Perkins Institute for the Blind.

_____ 2. Helen Keller was a deaf and blind girl.

_____ 3. She was seven.

_____ 4. Anne became Helen's teacher.

_____ 5. Helen was very undisciplined.

_____ 6. She was unable to communicate with her parents.

_____ 7. Anne was a great help to Helen.

_____ 8. She was patient with Helen.

_____ 9. Helen became a good student who could read Braille.

_____ 10. People were amazed at Anne's work.

_____ 11. Anne was proud when Helen graduated from college.

_____ 12. Her graduation was a great accomplishment.

_____ 13. Anne and Helen were happy to raise money for the American Foundation for the Blind.

_____ 14. They were a great success at giving lectures.

_____ 15. The two women were lifelong friends.

B. **Complete each sentence with a noun or an adjective used as a subject complement.**

1. My favorite food is _____.

2. I like that food because it is _____.

3. My least favorite food is _____.

4. I don't like that food because it is _____.

5. The best meal I ever ate was _____.

Sentences

113

108. Sentence Order

A sentence is in **natural order** when the verb follows the subject.

The little house stood on the prairie.

A sentence is in **inverted order** when the verb or a helping verb comes before the subject.

On the prairie stood the little house.

Underline the simple subject and circle the simple predicate. Write N if the sentence is in natural order and I if the sentence is in inverted order.

_____ 1. Many centuries ago lived the Anasazi.

_____ 2. *Anasazi* is a Navajo word meaning "ancient ones."

_____ 3. Some of their ruins are in Colorado's Mesa Verde National Park.

_____ 4. In the high cliffs of the Mesa Verde area they built cliff dwellings.

_____ 5. Four stories high stood some of these dwellings.

_____ 6. The Anasazi used ladders to enter their cliff homes.

_____ 7. In the winter, bitterly cold were these homes.

_____ 8. The Anasazi were called Basketmakers.

_____ 9. They excelled at basketry.

_____ 10. Waterproof were some of their baskets.

_____ 11. The archaeologists dug under the kiva, a community's underground room.

_____ 12. Through the kiva whipped the wind.

_____ 13. Below the cliff dwellings lies a trash area.

_____ 14. Piñon pines and juniper trees grew in the area.

_____ 15. The Anasazi farms lay on top of the mesa.

Name _____

109. Compound Subjects

> If a sentence has two or more simple subjects joined by a coordinating conjunction, it is said to have a **compound subject**.
>
> The <u>student</u> and the <u>teacher</u> discussed the assignment.

A. Read each sentence. Underline the compound subject. Circle the conjunction.

1. Grapes and peaches grow on that farm.

2. Fruits and vegetables are good sources of vitamins.

3. Not Brendan but Juan fed apples to the horses.

4. California and Florida have many orange groves.

5. Strawberries and rhubarb were the ingredients.

6. Carrots and sweet potatoes are orange.

7. My rabbits and my guinea pigs eat lettuce.

8. Insects or droughts can ruin vegetable crops.

9. Corn and pumpkins are sold at the roadside market.

10. Nicole and her family picked blueberries in Michigan.

11. Joan but not Phoebe brought a piece of fruit for lunch.

12. Cows and horses are kept in separate barns.

13. Ducks and geese swim in the pond near the farm.

14. Broccoli or carrots are good additions on a salad.

15. Corn and soybeans are the chief crops of Nebraska and Illinois.

B. Complete each sentence with a compound subject.

1. _____ and _____ have gone to the airport.

2. _____ and _____ are coming to visit.

3. The _____ and the _____ just fit in the trunk.

4. _____ and _____ will have lots to talk about.

5. _____ or _____ will take Grandpa for a walk.

Name _____

110. Compound Predicates

> If a sentence has two or more verbs joined by a conjunction, it is said to have a **compound predicate**.
>
> **A thief <u>stole</u> and <u>sold</u> the famous painting.**

A. Underline the compound simple predicate in each sentence. Circle the conjunction.

1. The patients sat and waited for the doctor.

2. Their friends and spouses cheered and comforted them.

3. The busy orderlies came and went through the emergency room doors.

4. Those doors opened and closed frequently.

5. The victim was calmed and then was examined by the doctors.

6. He yelled and cried in pain when they touched him.

7. The pregnant woman perspired and breathed hard during delivery.

8. The premature baby did not kick or scream as other babies do.

9. The mother nurses or feeds the baby with a bottle.

10. The father talks and sings to the baby.

B. Read the sentences. Combine each pair of sentences into one sentence with a compound predicate.

1. The teacher stacked the tests on her desk. She wrote the directions on the board.

_____

2. The student cleared his desk. The student sharpened his pencil.

_____

3. After the test put your pencils down. After the test turn your papers over.

_____

4. Now we'll review our tests. Now we'll correct our mistakes.

_____

5. The student reached for his test. The student smiled when he saw it.

_____

111. Compound Direct Objects

> If a verb has two or more direct objects, it is said to have
> a **compound direct object**.
>
> **In gym class we played basketball and floor hockey.**

A. Underline the compound direct object in each sentence.
Circle the conjunction.

1. We will visit the Sears Tower or the John Hancock Building
   in Chicago.

2. Visitors to New York can see the Statue of Liberty
   but not the Eiffel Tower.

3. In London buy a postcard or a model of Big Ben's clock
   tower, one of London's famous landmarks.

4. Venice's St. Mark's Square boasts many tourists and pigeons.

5. Can you envision Rome's Colosseum and Athens's Parthenon?

6. Photograph the Sphinx and the Great Pyramid when you tour Egypt.

7. Research Falling Water or Taliesin to find out about
   Frank Lloyd Wright's architecture.

8. Read the rules and regulations carefully before entering
   the Taj Mahal, a beautiful building in Agra, India.

9. The Eiffel Tower in Paris attracts many tourists but few locals.

10. See every nook and cranny of Sagrada Familia (Holy Family),
    a famous church in Barcelona, Spain.

B. Complete each sentence with a compound object.

1. Do you have a _____ or a _____?

2. I am writing a short _____ or a _____.

3. A writer needs _____ to write on or a _____
   to type on.

4. That topic makes _____ and _____ alike
   think seriously.

5. Ask a _____ or _____ to publish your work.

Sentences

117

112. Compound Subject Complements

A sentence with more than one subject complement has a **compound subject complement**. Noun subject complements rename the subject of the sentence. Adjective subject complements describe the subject.

Leonardo da Vinci was an <u>artist</u> and an <u>inventor</u>.
His paintings are <u>few</u> but <u>famous</u>.

A. Underline the compound subject complement in each sentence. Write **N** if the words are nouns or **A** if the words are adjectives.

_____ 1. As a boy Leonardo was handsome and charming.

_____ 2. He was a good singer and musician.

_____ 3. He was also a vegetarian and an animal lover.

_____ 4. At age 15 he became the helper and student of a painter.

_____ 5. Leonardo was creative and skillful.

_____ 6. Two of his famous paintings are *The Last Supper* and the *Mona Lisa*.

_____ 7. The models were people from Milan and a lady from Florence.

_____ 8. The smile on the *Mona Lisa* is small and mysterious.

_____ 9. Leonardo was an engineer and an architect.

_____ 10. His employers were governments and royalty.

_____ 11. His inventions were clever and astonishing.

_____ 12. Some of his projects were bridges and a mechanical lion.

_____ 13. Other ideas were a flying machine and a submarine.

_____ 14. In 1516 he became a painter and an architect for the King of France.

_____ 15. Leonardo's life was long and exciting.

B. Complete each sentence with a compound subject complement. Add articles if needed.

1. My favorite movies are _____ and _____.

2. My favorite kinds of TV shows are _____ and _____.

3. I would like to be _____ or _____.

4. When I work, I am _____ and _____.

5. My friends think I am _____ and _____.

113. Compound Sentences

A **compound sentence** contains two or more independent clauses. An independent clause has a subject and a predicate and can stand alone as a sentence. A compound sentence is formed by connecting two independent clauses with a comma and the coordinating conjunction *and, but,* or *or.* A semicolon (;) may be used instead of the comma and the conjunction.

Owls have large heads, and their eyes face forward.
Owls cannot move their eyes within their eye sockets; they must move their entire heads to look around.

A. For each of these compound sentences, draw one line under the complete subject in each independent clause and two lines under the complete predicate.

1. An owl's thick feathers absorb sound, and an owl's flight is almost silent.

2. Some owls have feathered ear tufts, but these tufts are not really ears.

3. Owls are carnivores, and most owls hunt at night.

4. An owl's keen sense of sight helps the owl navigate in the dark, and a sharp sense of hearing helps it find food.

5. Owls are at the top of a food chain; adult owls have few predators.

B. Combine each pair of sentences to make a compound sentence. Use a comma and a coordinating conjunction to combine the sentences.

1. Burrowing owls live in grasslands. These owls are unusual in many ways.

   _____

2. The owls are the size of robins. They are often active in broad daylight.

   _____

3. An adult burrowing owl is about nine inches tall. It has a short tail and long legs.

   _____

4. It has a rounded head. Unlike many other owls, it does not have ear tufts.

   _____

5. The burrowing owl's diet includes rodents, small birds, and eggs. It will also eat reptiles and insects.

   _____

Sentences

Name _____

114. Complex Sentences

A **complex sentence** contains one independent clause and one dependent clause. An independent clause has a subject and a predicate and can stand alone as a sentence. A dependent clause has a subject and a predicate but cannot stand alone as a sentence. A subordinate conjunction introduces a dependent clause and connects it to the independent clause. Many dependent clauses tell *when.* They are introduced by subordinate conjunctions such as *after, as, as soon as, before, once, since, when, whenever, while,* and *until.*

Few white people lived in the Dakota Territory when Crazy Horse was born. As Crazy Horse grew up, he earned a reputation for skill and daring.

Underline the independent clause in each complex sentence once. Underline the dependent clause twice. Circle the subordinate conjunction.

1. Before the Civil War was fought, the Sioux controlled a vast area of land.

2. Miners and prospectors moved to South Dakota's Black Hills after gold was discovered there.

3. As more settlers arrived, the U.S. War Department ordered the nomadic Sioux and Cheyenne to reservations.

4. When they heard the order, Crazy Horse and Sitting Bull refused to obey.

5. After a party of Sioux and Cheyenne defeated a band of U.S. soldiers, Lieutenant Colonel George A. Custer led an attack against the tribes.

6. When the battle was over, Custer and half of his men were dead.

7. The Army pursued the Indians until they were forced to surrender and move to a reservation.

8. When Crazy Horse's wife got sick, he took her to visit her parents at another reservation.

9. As soon as the soldiers heard that Crazy Horse had left, they followed him and arrested him.

10. Crazy Horse died after one of the soldiers stabbed him with a bayonet.

Crazy Horse stood up for what he believed in. Give an example of how you can stand up for what you believe.

Sentences

Name _____

115. Reviewing Sentences

A. Read each sentence. Write **CS** if the *italicized* words are a complete subject or **CP** if they are a complete predicate. Write your answers on the lines.

_____ 1. *A ferocious mile-wide tornado* descended upon the town.

_____ 2. Debris *swirled around its funnel cloud.*

_____ 3. Its loud roar *echoed in the night.*

_____ 4. Trees and buildings *were leveled by its winds.*

_____ 5. *Its massive force* tore homes into pieces.

B. Read each sentence. Write **S** on the line if the words form a sentence. Write **NS** on the line if the words do not form a sentence.

_____ 6. Skipping through the woods on a spring morning.

_____ 7. The wolf peered from behind a tree.

_____ 8. Each flower caught Little Red Riding Hood's attention.

_____ 9. A large bouquet for Grandmother.

_____ 10. To Grandmother's house she went.

C. Write on the line **declarative, interrogative, imperative,** or **exclamatory** to tell what kind of sentence is shown. Then underline the simple subject and circle the simple predicate. Remember that the subject of an imperative sentence is understood to be *you.*

_____ 11. Atalanta ran far ahead of Hippomenes.

_____ 12. Could Hippomenes possibly win?

_____ 13. Help me now, Venus.

_____ 14. The youth threw a golden apple far ahead.

_____ 15. Ah, it caught Atalanta's attention!

_____ 16. Would she pick up the apple?

_____ 17. Yes, Atalanta did!

_____ 18. Take advantage of this, Hippomenes.

_____ 19. Hippomenes and Atalanta were side by side.

_____ 20. Hippomenes aimed and threw the remaining apples.

D. Read each sentence. Write **CS** if the *italicized* words form a compound subject, **CP** if they form a compound predicate, or **CO** if they form a compound object. Write your answers on the lines.

Write **N** over the sentence if it is in natural order or **I** if it is in inverted order.

_____ 21. Inside Atalanta's mind fought good *judgment* and *foolishness*.

_____ 22. She *wavered* and *picked* them up.

_____ 23. Hippomenes saw *hope* and *victory* within his grasp.

_____ 24. He *reached* and *crossed* the finish line first.

_____ 25. He had won for himself a *race* and a *bride*!

Try It Yourself

Write four sentences about a game or contest you have seen. Be sure to use complete sentences and correct punctuation.

_____

_____

_____

_____

Check Your Own Work

Choose a selection from your writing portfolio, your journal, a work in progress, an assignment from another class, or a letter. Revise it, applying the skills you have reviewed. This checklist will help you.

✔ Do all your sentences express a complete thought?

✔ Have you used a variety of sentences—declarative, interrogative, imperative, and exclamatory?

Sentences

Name _____

116. End Punctuation

A declarative sentence makes a statement. An imperative sentence gives a command. Use a **period** at the end of a declarative or an imperative sentence. An interrogative sentence asks a question. Use a **question mark** at the end of an interrogative sentence. An exclamatory sentence expresses strong emotion. Use an **exclamation point** at the end of an exclamatory sentence.

> **Charles Dickens wrote *A Christmas Carol*.**
> **Please read it aloud.**
> **What happens to Tiny Tim?**
> **What a great story!**

Add the correct end punctuation to each sentence.

1. Charles Dickens is a well-known English author

2. When was he born

3. He was born in Portsmouth on February 7, 1812

4. What was his childhood like

5. His family was very poor

6. When he was 12, he had to get a job in a factory

7. How awful that was

8. In 1836 Dickens married Catherine Hogarth

9. The couple had 10 children

10. What a large family

11. What did Dickens do besides writing

12. He edited magazines and gave lectures

13. He had a lot of energy

14. He would often walk 30 miles

15. That's amazing

16. In 1842 Dickens visited the United States

17. What states did he visit

18. He traveled as far south as Virginia and as far west as Illinois

19. He wrote *American Notes* about his journey

20. Read one of his books for your book report

117. Commas in Series

Commas are used to separate three or more items in a series. A comma is placed before the coordinating conjunction at the end of the series. A series may consist of all nouns, all verbs, all adverbs, all adjectives, or all phrases.

Please pick up some bread, butter, and bananas at the store.
My mom, my dad, or my brother will cook dinner tonight.

A. Add commas where needed.

1. You should never skip breakfast lunch or dinner.
2. Mom used her Irish linen her German china and her English silver.
3. Jacob put cereal juice yogurt and bagels on the table.
4. Mom served cherry streusel banana cream pie and cheese coffeecake.
5. Quinn can prepare scrambled poached and hardboiled eggs.
6. In the picnic basket were sandwiches fruit pretzels and lemonade.
7. Dad bought carrots lettuce radishes and cucumbers for the salad.
8. The recipe said to chop mix season and cook the ingredients.
9. Celery lettuce and peppers are my favorite vegetables.
10. Martha stretched pulled kneaded and rolled out the dough.
11. Nathan Katie and Elizabeth will bring dessert for the picnic.
12. Is the bread on the counter in the cupboard or in the refrigerator?
13. My sisters my mother and my aunts are all excellent cooks.
14. The recipe says to stir the mixture slowly carefully and thoroughly.
15. The plums are sweet juicy and delicious.

B. Complete each sentence with a series of nouns, verbs, or adjectives. Add commas where needed.

1. _____ _____ and _____ are my favorite rides at the amusement park.
2. I saw _____ _____ and _____ at the fairgrounds.
3. Did you _____ _____ or _____ at the beach?
4. The water slide was _____ _____ and _____ .
5. In the winter I _____ _____ and _____ for fun.

118. Commas with Conjunctions

Commas are used before the conjunctions *and*, *but*, and *or* when two simple sentences are combined.

Some of the children went to art class, but others went to the gym.

A. Read each sentence. Add commas where needed.

1. Marie likes to use paint for her art and Erica likes to use pastels.

2. She redrew the figure but it still wasn't right.

3. We will finish our paintings in class or we will finish them at home.

4. The critic didn't like her drawings but he liked her sculptures.

5. They put their paints away and then they cleaned their brushes.

B. Read each sentence. Use a conjunction to complete each sentence. Add commas where needed.

1. Fold your paper into four equal parts _____ then you can draw a favorite book character in each section.

2. I will draw Huck Finn in one of the sections _____ I don't know who will go in the other sections.

3. Huck had a friend named Jim _____ was his name John?

4. Read *Huckleberry Finn* _____ you will miss a good story.

5. Mark Twain wrote *Huckleberry Finn* _____ that is not all he wrote.

C. Combine each set of simple sentences with a conjunction. Add commas where needed.

1. There was a long wait to ride the roller coaster. You could get on the bumper cars immediately.

_____

2. Don't eat too much food. You might feel ill on the rides.

_____

3. We ate lunch. Then we went on the train ride.

_____

4. Henry's favorite ride is the Wild Eagle. Julia enjoys the Twirly Whirly.

_____

5. The Wild Eagle is fun. The Twirly Whirly can be scary.

_____

Punctuation and Capitalization

125

119. Direct Address and Yes and No

Commas are used to separate words in direct address. When the name of a person addressed is the first word of a sentence, it is followed by a comma. If it is the last word of a sentence, a comma is placed before the name.

> **Tony, let's go.**   **What is this thing, Sarah?**

If the name of the person is used within a sentence, one comma is placed before the name and one after the name.

> **I hope you know, Gina, how much I appreciate your help.**

Commas are used after the words *yes* and *no* when either introduces a sentence.

> **Yes, you may go bike riding.**   **No, it's too late to go out.**

A.   Read each sentence. Add commas where needed.

1. Yes seals and penguins can be found in Antarctic waters.
2. Seals Jackie have a layer of fat that keeps them warm in cold water.
3. Did you read the chapter on animals of the Antarctic Kevin?
4. Boys and girls can you name some kinds of seals?
5. No not all seals have external ears.
6. Trina the female seal is called a cow.
7. Can you tell me what the male seal is called class?
8. Yes the male seal is called a bull.
9. Usually Eric the cow has just one pup per breeding season.
10. Yes the leopard seal sometimes feeds on penguins.
11. Penguins live in groups called rookeries Paige.
12. The male penguins David hold the eggs on their feet.
13. No the females do not guard the eggs.
14. Yes penguins are heavy birds.
15. That makes them good divers and swimmers Colette.

B.   Complete each sentence with a noun in direct address. Use correct punctuation.

1. Ernest Shackleton _____ explored the South Pole.
2. His ship was called the *Endurance* _____ .
3. The *Endurance* _____ got trapped in the ice.
4. Eventually _____ the ship was crushed by the ice and sank.
5. _____ can you imagine being stranded in a lifeboat in those icy waters?

Name _____

120. Apostrophes

> An **apostrophe** is used to show ownership or possession. To show that one person or thing owns something, place an apostrophe and an *s* ('s) after a singular noun. To show that more than one person or thing owns something, place an apostrophe after the *s* at the end of a regular plural noun. If a plural noun does not end in *-s,* place an apostrophe and an *s* ('s) after the noun.
>
> **The boy's bicycle is in the bike rack.**
> **The girls' bicycles are in the bike rack.**
> **The women's bicycles are in the bike rack.**
>
> An **apostrophe** is used in a contraction to indicate where a letter or letters have been omitted.
>
> **She's aware that I'm waiting for her.**

A. Write the correct possessive form of the word to complete each sentence. Singular possessives are needed in some sentences, and plural possessives in others.

child 1. The three _____ trip to Everglades National Park was exciting.

park 2. Both alligators and crocodiles live in the _____ swamps.

alligator 3. Many _____ nests lie among the roots of mangrove trees.

alligator 4. An _____ nest is a mound of vegetation.

crocodile 5. Most _____ eggs are laid in mud or sand.

crocodile 6. They saw a _____ eyes just above the water.

ibis 7. A white _____ bill is long and curved.

Ibis 8. _____ favorite food is crayfish.

Human 9. _____ attempts to manage the water in south Florida have endangered the Everglades.

animal 10. Many _____ habitats are disappearing.

B. Write the contraction for each pair of words.

1. does not _____
2. are not _____
3. did not _____
4. will not _____
5. we have _____

6. I will _____
7. we will _____
8. you have _____
9. I have _____
10. you are _____

121. Capital Letters

> The first word of every sentence begins with a **capital letter**. A proper noun begins with a capital letter. A proper noun names a particular person, place, or thing.
>
> the first national park in the united states was yellowstone national park.
> The first national park in the United States was Yellowstone National Park.

A. Use the proofreading symbol (≡) under letters that should be capitalized.

1. in 1871 ferdinand hayden led an expedition through the wyoming territory.

2. the artist thomas moran and the photographer william henry jackson accompanied him.

3. their pictures convinced congress that yellowstone should be preserved.

4. president grant signed a law in 1872 to protect yellowstone forever.

5. yellowstone is located in idaho, montana, and wyoming.

6. the most famous geyser in yellowstone is old faithful.

7. one of the smallest national parks is acadia national park in maine.

8. acadia, the first national park east of the mississippi river, was originally called lafayette national park.

9. president woodrow wilson signed legislation in 1919 that established the park.

10. acadia offers mountain hiking with views of the atlantic ocean.

11. the largest national park is wrangell–saint elias.

12. this park, located in alaska, is six times the size of yellowstone.

13. tourists to wrangell–saint elias can visit kennecott, an old copper mining town.

14. at hawaii's volcanoes national park you can see kilauea, one of the most active volcanoes in the world.

15. the kilauea cultural festival gives hawaiians an opportunity to honor their culture and traditions.

B. Circle the groups of words that are capitalized correctly.

1. Princeton university

2. the Boy Scouts

3. Mother's day

4. Ashland Avenue

5. the White House

6. Jacqueline Bouvier Kennedy

7. the Mississippi river

8. south Dakota

9. the National Air and Space Museum

10. Colorado springs, Colorado

122. Titles

A capital letter is used for the first letter of each important word in the title of a book, movie, TV show, play, poem, song, artwork, sacred book, article, or essay. Articles, prepositions, and conjunctions are not usually capitalized. The first and last words of a title are always capitalized.

Quotation marks are used to enclose the titles of short stories, poems, and magazine articles.

STORY	"The Scarlet Ibis"
POEM	"The Other Side of the Door"

Titles of most books, magazines, plays, movies, and works of art are typed in italics. When you write the title of a book or work of art, underline the title since you cannot write in italics.

BOOK	*The Secret Garden*	The Secret Garden
MOVIE	*Star Wars*	Star Wars
PAINTING	*Starry Night*	Starry Night

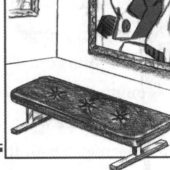

A. Add the proofreading mark (≡) to show which letters should be capitalized.

1. Have you read the poem "tug of war" by Kathleen Fraser?

2. Let's watch teen talent show on television tonight.

3. *the seeing summer* is a beautiful book about a blind girl.

4. Which artist painted *whistling boy*?

5. "valentine for earth" is a delightful poem by Frances Frost.

6. I enjoyed reading the short story "bowleg bill, cowboy of the ocean waves."

7. Does the library have the book *old yeller*?

8. Draw a picture after you have read the poem "subways are people."

9. The girl in the painting *girl with watering can* looks like my little sister.

10. My uncle is directing a production of the play *a raisin in the sun*.

B. Complete each sentence with appropriate information, capitalizing important words. Add quotation marks and underlining where needed.

1. _____ is my favorite book.

2. Do you like the poem _____?

3. My favorite TV show is _____.

4. Our class went to the museum and saw the painting _____.

5. I just finished reading the story _____.

123. Other Uses of Capital Letters

A capital letter is used for the first word in a direct quotation; the directions North, South, East, and West when they refer to specific regions of a country; the pronoun *I*; titles that precede a person's name; and initials in a person's name.

Mom said, "We are going to tour the South on our vacation."
Did you know that Sir Winston Churchill's mother was an American?

A. Rewrite each phrase, using the correct capitalization.

1. famous cities of the south _____

2. president george h. w. bush _____

3. my cousins and i _____

4. animals of the north _____

5. chief justice warren e. burger _____

6. queen elizabeth II _____

7. doctor benjamin spock _____

8. women of the west _____

9. j. k. rowling _____

10. madame c. j. walker _____

B. Use the proofreading symbol (≡) to show which letters should be capitalized.

1. last spring my dad said, "let's drive to the east this summer."

2. "great," my mom answered, "i have always wanted to go to washington, d.c."

3. as soon as we had decided to go, i started doing research.

4. we can hear jazz at the john f. kennedy center.

5. my brother and i want to visit the building where the supreme court meets.

6. my dad said, "i want to see the jefferson memorial."

7. he admires president jefferson for sending lewis and clark to explore the west.

8. we will be able to go to the top of the washington monument.

9. this monument honors president george washington.

10. Finally we will visit the graves of robert e. peary and matthew a. henson, two famous explorers, at arlington national cemetery.

124. Abbreviations

An **abbreviation** is a shortened form of a word. Use a period after many abbreviations. Capital letters are used for abbreviations when capital letters would be used if the words were written in full.

Reverend	Rev.	Senior	Sr.
Sunday	Sun.	January	Jan.
Street	St.	foot	ft.
before Christ	BC	after noon	p.m.

The abbreviations for terms in the metric system do not begin with capital letters and are not followed by periods. The postal abbreviations for the states have two capital letters and are not followed by periods.

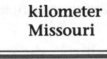

meter		kilometer	km
Illinois		Missouri	MO

A. Write the abbreviation for each of these words.

1. November _____
2. gallon _____
3. Avenue _____
4. Doctor _____
5. centimeter _____

6. ounce _____
7. quart _____
8. Junior _____
9. yard _____
10. Wednesday _____

B. Rewrite each sentence. Use abbreviations whenever possible.

1. On Thursday, August 11, Doctor Irwin Stone, Junior, visited the Sears Tower.

_____

2. The building is located at 233 South Wacker Drive, Chicago, Illinois.

_____

3. It is 1,454 feet, or about one-quarter mile, tall.

_____

4. Piles driven into the earth support the tower's 440 million pounds.

_____

5. The Sears Tower contains enough concrete to build an eight-lane highway five miles long.

_____

125. Direct Quotations

A **direct quotation** restates the exact words a person has spoken. Quotation marks are used before and after a direct quotation.

> **"We have more of these in stock," offered the salesperson.**

When a direct quotation comes at the beginning of the sentence, a comma is placed after the quotation.

> **"The story had interesting characters," remarked Lucy.**

When a direct quotation comes at the end of the sentence, a comma is placed before the quotation.

> **The police officer warned, "Wear your seatbelts at all times."**

If the quotation ends with a question mark or exclamation point, the comma is not used.

> **"Must you wear that dirty sweatshirt?" she asked.**
> **"I won the prize!" cried Michael.**

A. **Add quotation marks and other punctuation where needed.**

1. Who wants to go to the botanical gardens? inquired William.

2. I would like to see the spring flowers there replied his sister Lindsay.

3. Let's get in the car Mom said.

4. Buckle your seat belts instructed Mom.

5. This plant is quite fragile cautioned the botanist.

6. Lindsay remarked It's beautiful!

7. Where does it grow? asked William.

8. The botanist answered It grows primarily on the Pacific islands.

9. William questioned Like Hawaii?

10. Yes, it is very common there said the botanist.

B. **Complete each sentence with the exact words of the speaker. Add quotation marks and punctuation where needed.**

1. _____ shouted the referee.

2. Miguel announced _____ .

3. Emily asked _____ .

4. _____ pleaded the class.

5. _____ said the teacher.

126. More Direct Quotations

Quotation marks are used before and after every part of a divided quotation. When the exact words of the speaker are divided, more than one comma is used to separate the quotation from the rest of the sentence. Use a capital letter before the first word of a quotation, but do not use a capital letter where the quotation continues.

"King Montezuma," said the guide, "drank 50 cups of chocolate a day."

A question mark or an exclamation point that is part of the direct quotation is placed inside the quotation marks. When a question mark or an exclamation point is not part of the quotation, it is placed outside the quotation marks.

Was it Patrick Henry who said, "Give me liberty or give me death!"?
Yes, it was he who exclaimed, "Give me liberty or give me death!"

A. **Add quotation marks and punctuation where needed.**

1. This is not Paul muttered my favorite pastime.

2. Oh, really asked Gillian what would you rather be doing?

3. I'd much rather be outside on my bike responded Paul.

4. Gillian asked Paul wouldn't you rather be doing something else too?

5. Sure I would said Gillian but we promised Mom we'd help her get ready for the party.

6. Right agreed Paul we sure did.

7. Do you think asked Paul that we've cut up enough vegetables?

8. Yes, said Gillian I think that we've prepared enough for the tray.

9. Now what we need to do stated Paul is make the dip.

10. No returned Gillian I've already made it.

B. **Complete each sentence with the exact words of the speaker. Add quotation marks and punctuation where needed.**

1. _____ Joseph explained _____

2. _____ announced Anna _____

3. _____ said Darnell _____

4. _____ encouraged the coach _____

5. _____ the butcher replied _____

127. Addresses and Letters

In an address, capitalize the name and title of the person addressed; the name of the street and the city or town; both letters in the state's postal abbreviation; and abbreviations such as *N.* for *North,* *S.* for *South,* *E.* for *East,* and *W.* for *West.* Use a comma after the name of the city or town.

Capitalize the first word of the salutation and the first word in the complimentary close of a letter. Use a comma after the salutation of a personal letter and a colon after the salutation of a business letter. Use a comma after the closing.

2700 W. Maple Grove Ave.
Missoula, MT 59804
May 19, 20—

Barton Conners
Director of Advertising
3660 Austrian Lane
Green Bay, WI 54302

A. **Rewrite each phrase, adding capital letters and punctuation where needed.**

1. dear uncle charley _____

2. all my best _____

3. sincerely yours _____

4. dear mrs pinkley _____

5. january 27 2006 _____

B. **Rewrite each address, adding capital letters and punctuation where needed.**

1. dr charles j warner _____
   stickly research lab _____
   3659 old mill road _____
   canton oh 44707 _____

2. laura phelps _____
   gateway seed company _____
   4445 w ash street _____
   bangor me 04401 _____

3. doug yee, jr _____
   skateboards plus _____
   36 e grand ave _____
   petaluma ca 94952 _____

128. Reviewing Punctuation and Capitalization

A. **Add periods where needed.**

1. M C Johnson began a new business

2. Nov is the abbreviation for November

3. What famous battle occurred in AD 1066?

4. Dr Horn arrived at the hospital at 3:55 a m

5. Workers at the Pennsboro Electric Co went on strike today

B. **Write the correct abbreviation for each word.**

6. Tuesday _____ 11. August _____

7. liter _____ 12. Avenue _____

8. Captain _____ 13. foot _____

9. pint _____ 14. Wednesday _____

10. Mister _____ 15. inch _____

C. **Add commas where needed. Use the proofreading symbol (≡) under letters that should be capitalized.**

16. our first three presidents were washington adams and jefferson.

17. on september 17 1796 washington delivered his famous farewell address.

18. "do not count your chickens before they are hatched" aesop advised.

19. yes the dead sea is the saltiest.

20. do you want a sandwich dan?

D. **Add exclamation points, question marks, and apostrophes where needed.**

21. Hurrah The storm is over.

22. How much damage did it do

23. Im going to help our neighbors.

24. My fathers house was not damaged.

25. What a terrible 20 minutes that was

CONTINUED

E. Add quotation marks where needed.

26. Have you read *Oliver Twist* by Dickens? asked Colleen.

27. No, said Martina, but I would like to read it.

28. Will you tell me about it? she asked.

29. Oliver, said Colleen, was a poor orphan boy.

30. She continued, He became involved with criminals in London.

F. Add quotation marks or underlining where needed.

31. Charles Dickens also wrote the novel Great Expectations.

32. My mother loves that book and a play called The Frozen Deep in which Dickens acted.

33. She also appreciates great art, such as Van Gogh's The Potato Eaters.

34. Death Be Not Proud is her favorite poem.

35. She wrote her short story Awaken based on it.

Try It Yourself

Write four sentences about one of your favorite books.
Be sure to use capital letters and punctuation marks correctly.

_____

_____

_____

_____

Check Your Own Work

Choose a selection from your writing portfolio, your journal, a work in progress, an assignment from another class, or a letter. Revise it, applying the skills you have reviewed. This checklist will help you.

✔ Do your sentences end with the right punctuation marks?

✔ Have you followed the rules for commas?

✔ Have you used apostrophes and quotation marks correctly?

✔ Have you capitalized all proper nouns and proper adjectives?

129. Subjects, Predicates, Direct Objects, Modifiers

A **diagram** shows how the words in a sentence fit together. It highlights the most important words in a sentence and shows how the other words relate to them.

SENTENCE: **The hungry children quickly ate the green grapes.**

Start the diagram by drawing a horizontal line. Find the verb in the sentence and write it in the middle of the line. Find the simple subject and write it in front of the verb. Draw a vertical line between the subject and the verb. The vertical line should cut through the horizontal line.

    children | ate

Now find the direct object in the sentence. Write the direct object on the horizontal line to the right of the verb. Draw a vertical line between the verb and the direct object. This line touches the horizontal line but does not cut through it.

    children | ate | grapes

Words that describe the subject, the verb, or the direct object are written on slanting lines under those words.

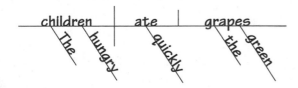

Diagram each of these sentences.

1. My mom made a delicious lunch.

2. The band played my favorite song.

3. I carefully planted the tiny seeds.

4. The clever girl performed several magic tricks.

5. The puppy wagged its tail happily.

6. The sleepy children slowly climbed the stairs.

7. Linda's dad quickly fixed her bike.

8. The black horse easily jumped the low fence.

130. Indirect Objects

In a diagram an indirect object is placed on a horizontal line beneath the verb. It is connected to the verb by a slanted line. Words that describe the indirect object go on slanting lines under the indirect object.

SENTENCE: **The teacher gave the students their grades.**

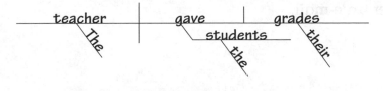

Diagram each of these sentences.

1. Henry's mom made the boys some lemonade.

2. The same reporter asked the mayor a question.

3. The babysitter read the sleepy children a story.

4. My cousin sold me his old telescope.

CONTINUED

Diagramming

5. I happily showed my mother my latest painting.

6. Tom is writing his older brother an e-mail.

7. The coach handed the players their new uniforms.

8. The ringmaster offered the elephant a peanut.

9. My little sister owes me five dollars.

10. The waiter handed each hungry diner a menu.

131. Subject Complements

In a diagram a subject complement is written on the main horizontal line after the verb. A line that slants back toward the subject separates the subject complement and the verb. The slanting line touches the horizontal line but does not cut through it.

SENTENCE: **That tall man is the basketball coach.**

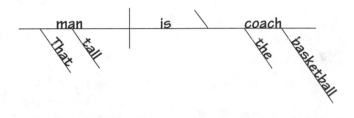

Diagram each of these sentences.

1. Crisp, juicy apples are my favorite fruit.

2. The skater's tricks were difficult.

3. The short blond boy is the fastest runner.

4. My dad is a great cook.

5. Gloria's new skateboard is orange.

6. That TV show was wonderful.

7. George Washington was our first president.

8. Tomorrow could be your lucky day.

9. Lee Ann's wooden sculpture was impressive.

10. The singer's final note was flat.

132. Prepositional Phrases

In a diagram a prepositional phrase goes beneath the word it describes. The preposition is on a slanting line. The object of the preposition is on a horizontal line that connects to the slanting line. Any word or words that describe the object go on slanting lines under the object.

SENTENCE: **The woman in the red hat gave me a look of total joy.**

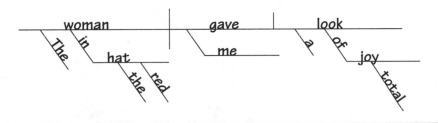

Diagram each of these sentences.

1. The tops of the trees swayed in the wind.

2. My cousin was the winner of the race.

3. Bristlecone pines are the oldest living things on earth.

4. The boy on the green bike told his friends a story about a pirate.

Diagramming

5. The members of the orchestra played several pieces by Mozart.

6. Abraham Lincoln was president during the Civil War.

7. After dinner I walked to my friend's house.

8. The aliens in the movie frightened the children in the audience.

9. The driver gave the reporter from the newspaper a full account of the accident.

133. Interjections

In a diagram an interjection is placed on a line that is separate from the rest of the sentence. The line is above, at the left of, and parallel to the main horizontal line.

Sentence: Help! The dog is eating my homework.

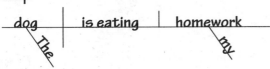

Diagram each of these sentences.

1. Oh, no! Your sister fell into that muddy puddle.

2. Yikes! I almost forgot Mario's birthday!

3. Yuck! Who made this pickle smoothie?

4. Oh! The flowers in your garden are beautiful.

CONTINUED

5. Our team won the pennant! Hooray!

6. Sh! The puppies are sleeping in their basket.

7. Uh-oh! I saw a skunk in the backyard.

8. Wow! My sister won first prize in the science fair!

9. Ouch! I poked my finger with the needle!

134. Compound Subjects and Compound Predicates

In a diagram each part of a compound subject or a compound verb is placed on a separate horizontal line. The coordinating conjunction is placed on a dashed line between the two horizontal lines. The lines are connected to the main horizontal line in the usual position of a subject or a verb.

SENTENCE: **Aaron and Melinda washed and dried the dishes.**

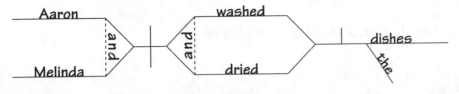

Diagram each of these sentences.

1. The players and the coach celebrated the victory.

2. Mom steamed zucchini and made fish tacos.

3. Sequoias and redwoods are interesting trees.

4. Lions and tigers live on separate continents.

Diagramming

5. The children collected cans and took them to the recycling center.

6. Mark and Melissa fed the dog and watered the plants.

7. Jenny washed and styled her sister's hair.

8. A bluebird or a sparrow built a nest in the birdhouse.

9. Mom gave me a ukulele and taught me a few songs.

10. Mysteries and science fiction are Carlo's favorite kinds of books.

135. Compound Direct Objects and Indirect Objects

In a diagram each part of a compound object is placed on a separate horizontal line. The coordinating conjunction is placed on a dashed line between the two horizontal lines. A compound direct object is connected to the main horizontal line and separated from the verb by a vertical line. A compound indirect object is placed under the verb with a slanted line connecting the indirect objects to the main horizontal line.

SENTENCE: **Aunt Clara gave my sister and me lemonade and cookies.**

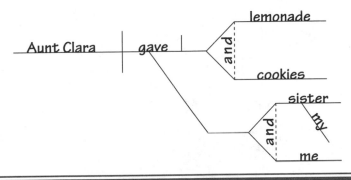

Diagram each of these sentences.

1. Dave took his guitar and his harmonica to the party.

2. The director of the show gave the actors and the musicians their instructions.

3. Owls often eat mice and other small rodents.

CONTINUED

Diagramming

4. The scientist told the interviewer and the audience the results of the experiment.

5. The league awarded the winner and the runner-up some trophies and other prizes.

6. The incident taught Kathy and Nate an important lesson about friendship.

7. The art teacher gave Sandy and Chris a box of paints and some brushes.

8. We sent the mayor and the governor letters about our recycling plan.

Name _____

136. Compound Subject Complements

In a diagram each part of a compound subject complement is placed on a separate horizontal line. The coordinating conjunction is placed on a dashed line between the two horizontal lines. The compound subject complement is connected to the main horizontal line and separated from the verb by a line that slants left.

SENTENCE: **The calm surface of the lake looked cool and inviting.**

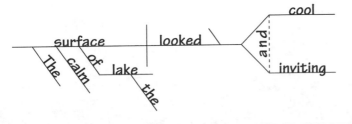

Diagram each of these sentences.

1. The new president of our class will be Connie or Nick.

2. The trees around the small pond were tall and shady.

3. My favorite subjects in school are history and math.

Diagramming

4. The only things in the weedy yard were an old shoe and a bicycle wheel.

5. A porcupine's quills are sharp and stiff.

6. The main characters in the story were Pecos Bill and his horse.

7. After the game the players were dirty and exhausted.

8. Grandma's famous grits are always cheesy and smooth.

137. Compound Sentences

In a diagram each clause in a compound sentence is placed on its own horizontal line and diagrammed separately. The coordinating conjunction is placed on a dashed vertical line that connects the left edges of the horizontal lines.

SENTENCE: **Chad lost his cell phone, and he hasn't found it anywhere.**

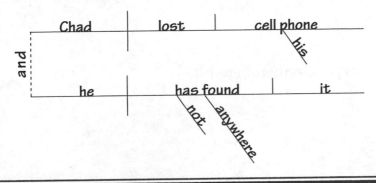

Diagram each of these sentences.

1. The weather was sunny yesterday, but it is cool and rainy today.

2. I made the sandwiches, and my sister washed the fruit.

3. The reporter asked the quarterback a question, but he walked away.

CONTINUED

4. I might watch TV after dinner, or I might write my friend an e-mail.

5. Lincoln's speech was short, but everyone remembered it.

6. The goalie deflected the shot, and our team won the game.

7. My mom offered me a snack, but I wasn't very hungry.

Name _____

138. Adverb Clauses

In a diagram an adverb clause is placed on a horizontal line under the horizontal line for the independent clause. Each clause is diagrammed separately. The subordinate conjunction is placed on a slanted dashed line that connects the verb in the adverb clause to the word in the independent clause that the adverb clause describes. It usually goes to the verb.

SENTENCE: **As the pioneers crossed the prairie, they faced many hardships.**

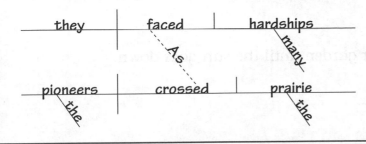

Diagram each of these sentences.

1. When the scientists found the fossils, they called the museum.

2. I wrote my senator a letter as soon as I heard the news.

3. They will go to the movie after they finish their homework.

CONTINUED

Diagramming

4. Before Joe and Nancy grilled the hamburgers, they sliced the tomatoes and the onions.

5. Mrs. Chan will work in her flower garden until the sun goes down.

6. The children get excited whenever they see a parade.

7. We heard the loud crash while we were riding our bikes.

139. Diagramming Review

In a diagram each part of a sentence has its own place.

Diagram each of these sentences.

1. Benjamin Franklin was a scientist and an inventor, and he published a famous almanac.

2. After my cousin went to college, my sister and I often sent her cards.

3. *Tyrannosaurus rex* had huge jaws and was a fierce predator.

4. My family and I visited Texas in the spring when the wildflowers were blooming.

CONTINUED

Diagramming

5. Micky is usually the best fielder on the team, but he dropped the fly ball.

6. Mount Rushmore is a national monument and a popular tourist destination.

7. Bison are the largest mammals in North America, and some Native Americans raise the giant animals for food.

8. The car's engine coughed and sputtered until my dad and my uncle fixed it.

Handbook of Terms

ADJECTIVES

An **adjective** is a word that describes a noun or pronoun.

Articles point out nouns. *A, an,* and *the* are articles.

- *A* and *an* are the indefinite articles. An indefinite article refers to any of a class of things: *a* banana, *an* elephant. *The* is the definite article. The definite article refers to one or more specific things: *A* pear and *an* apple are in *the* blue bowl.

- When two or more nouns joined by *and* name different people, places, or things, use an article before each noun. When two or more nouns joined by *and* refer to the same person, place, or thing, use an article before the first noun only: *The* singer and *the* dancer performed together. *The* actor and comedian is my cousin.

Demonstrative adjectives point out specific persons, places, or things.

- *This* and *that* point out one person, place, or thing.

- *These* and *those* point out more than one person, place, or thing.

- *This* and *these* point out persons, places, or things that are near.

- *That* and *those* point out persons, places, or things that are farther away.

Descriptive adjectives tell about the size, shape, color, weight, or other qualities of the things they describe. A descriptive adjective can come before a noun: *sunny* morning, *hot* day. A descriptive adjective can follow a linking verb: The sun is *warm*.

Interrogative adjectives are used in questions. An interrogative adjective goes before a noun. The interrogative adjectives are *what, which,* and *whose*: *What* types of books do you enjoy? *Which* book is your favorite? *Whose* book is this?

Possessive adjectives show possession or ownership. A possessive adjective goes before a noun. The possessive adjectives are *my, your* (singular or plural), *his, her, its, our,* and *their*: *his* skateboard, *their* bikes.

Proper adjectives are adjectives that come from proper nouns. A proper adjective begins with a capital letter: *American* history.

Some adjectives tell exactly how many: *ten, twenty-five, third, twelfth.* Some adjectives tell about how many: *many, few, several, some.*

See also **comparisons, prepositions, sentences.**

ADVERBS

An **adverb** is a word that describes a verb, an adjective, or another adverb.

- An **adverb of time** answers the question *when* or *how often:* It rained *yesterday.* We *usually* eat lunch at noon.

- An **adverb of place** answers the question *where:* Toshi bent his head *forward.* Sit *here* by the gate.

- An **adverb of manner** answers the question *how* or *in what manner:* Jason draws *well.* She dances the waltz *gracefully.*

Like adjectives, some adverbs can be used to compare.

- The **positive degree** of an adverb is the base form: Jonathan skates *quickly.*

- The **comparative degree** compares two actions and is often used with *than:* Jonathan skates *less quickly* than I skate.

- The **superlative degree** compares three or more actions: Jonathan skates *least quickly* of all his relatives.

A negative idea is expressed by using one negative word. That negative word may be *no, not, none, never,* or *nothing.* Those words should be used only in sentences that have no other negative words: I do not have *any* (not *no*) apples.

See also **clauses, comparisons, prepositions.**

ANTECEDENTS

The word to which a pronoun refers is its **antecedent.** The pronoun must agree with its antecedent in person and number. The third person singular must also show whether it refers to a male, a female, or a thing: *Jay* did as *he* was told.

CAPITALIZATION

Many words begin with a capital letter, including the following:

- the first word of a sentence—The bell rang.

- an abbreviation if the word it stands for begins with a capital letter—U.S. government

- titles that precede a person's name—Sir Paul McCartney

- the first word and the name of the person addressed in the salutation of a letter and the first word in the closing of a letter—Dear Marie, Yours truly,

- the first word, the last word, and each important word in the titles of books, plays, works of art, and poems—*A Tale of Two Cities, Romeo and Juliet, Starry Night,* "Fire and Ice"

- the first word of a direct quotation—Mother said, "It's time for my favorite television program."

- proper nouns and proper adjectives—America, American flag

- North, East, South, and West when they refer to a section of the country or the world—the old West. They are not capitalized when they refer to direction—He drove west on Main Street.

- names referring to the deity or to sacred books—God, the Bible

Capital letters are also used for:

- the pronoun *I*

- two-letter state postal abbreviations—MA, NY, CA

- initials in a person's name—I. M. Pei for Ieoh Ming Pei

CLAUSES

A **clause** is a group of words that has a subject and a predicate.

An **adverb clause** is a dependent clause used as an adverb. An adverb clause often answers the question *when:* We ate dinner *before we went to the movie.*

A **dependent clause** does not express a complete thought and cannot stand on its own as a sentence: *before we went to the movie.*

An **independent clause** expresses a complete thought and can stand on its own as a sentence: *We ate dinner.*

COMPARISONS

Many adjectives can be used to compare two or more persons, places, or things.

- An adjective in the **positive degree** describes one or more persons, places, or things: *quiet, powerful, attractive.*

- An adjective in the **comparative degree** compares two persons, places, or things. Form comparative adjectives by adding *-er* to the positive degree or by putting *more* or *less* before the positive degree: *quieter, more powerful, less attractive.*

- An adjective in the **superlative degree** compares three or more persons, places, or things. Form superlative adjectives by adding *-est* to the positive degree or by putting *most* or *least* before the positive degree: *quietest, most powerful, least attractive.*

Fewer and *fewest* refer to number; use them with plural count nouns: There are *fewer* apples than oranges. *Less* and *least* refer to quantity; use them with noncount nouns: My car uses *less* gas than yours.

Some adverbs can be used to compare two or more actions. Those adverbs have positive, comparative, and superlative degrees just as adjectives have.

- Form the comparative degree by adding *-er* to the positive degree or by putting *more* or *less* before the positive degree: *faster, more carefully, less slowly.*

- Form the superlative degree by adding *-est* to the positive degree or by putting *most* or *least* before the positive degree: *fastest, most carefully, least slowly.*

CONJUNCTIONS

A **conjunction** is a word used to connect words or groups of words.

A **coordinating conjunction** connects words or groups of words that are of equal importance. The most common coordinating conjunctions are *and, but,* and *or:* Joshua *and* Leanne cut *and* glued the words *and* the pictures on some posters, *and* Nancy took orders.

A **subordinate conjunction** introduces a dependent clause and connects it to an independent clause. Many subordinate conjunctions tell *when.* They include *after, as, as soon as, before, once, since, when, whenever, while,* and *until:* I'll help you *after* I finish my homework.

CONTRACTIONS

A **contraction** is two words written as one word with one or more letters omitted. An apostrophe (') is used to show the omission of a letter or letters. Subject pronouns are used with some verbs to form contractions: *we're* for *we are, she's* for *she is* or *she has.*

INTERJECTIONS

An **interjection** expresses a strong feeling or emotion. An interjection is followed by an exclamation mark: *Wow! Yikes!*

NOUNS

A **noun** is a name word. It names a person, place, or thing. A noun can be used as the subject, the direct object, the indirect object, the object of a preposition, or the subject complement in a sentence.

A **collective noun** names a group of persons, places, or things that are considered as a unit: The *band* played loudly.

A **common noun** names any one member of a group of persons, places, or things: *queen, city, church.*

Count nouns name items that can be counted separately. A count noun has a singular form and a plural form: *cherries, emotions, chairs.*

A noun is used in **direct address** when it names the person spoken to: *Carol,* would you help me?

Noncount nouns name items that cannot be counted separately. A noncount noun generally takes a verb that agrees with *he, she,* or *it.* A noncount noun does not have a plural form: *fruit, anger, furniture.*

A **plural noun** names more than one person, place, or thing: *boys, rivers, berries.*

A **possessive noun** expresses possession or ownership. The apostrophe (') is the sign of a possessive noun.

- To form the possessive of a singular noun, add *-'s* to the singular form: *architect's*

- To form the possessive of a plural noun that ends in *-s*, add an apostrophe to the plural form: *farmers'*

- To form the possessive of a plural noun that does not end in *-s*, add *-'s* to the plural form: *children's*

A **proper noun** names a particular person, place, or thing. A proper noun is capitalized: *Queen Elizabeth, London, Westminster Abbey.*

A **singular noun** names one person, place, or thing: *boy, river, berry.*

PREPOSITIONS

A **preposition** is a word that shows the relationship between a noun or a pronoun and another word in a sentence. The noun or pronoun that follows the preposition is the **object of the proposition:** The huge mountain lion leaped *through* (preposition) the tall *grass* (object of the preposition).

A **prepositional phrase** is a phrase that is introduced by a preposition.

- An **adjective phrase** is used as an adjective and describes a noun: The cabin *in the woods* burned down.

- An **adverb phrase** is used as an adverb and usually describes a verb: The river flows *into the sea.*

PRONOUNS

A **pronoun** is a word that takes the place of a noun or nouns.

Demonstrative pronouns point out people, places, and things. The singular demonstrative pronouns are *this* and *that.* The plural demonstrative pronouns are *these* and *those. This* and *these* point out things that are near *These* are my marbles here. *That* and *those* point out things that are farther away: *That* is my house over there.

An **intensive pronoun** is used to emphasize the noun that comes before it. The intensive pronouns are *myself, yourself, himself, herself, itself, ourselves, yourselves,* and *themselves:* He *himself* baked the pie.

An **interrogative pronoun** is used to ask a question. The interrogative pronouns are *who, whom, what,* and *whose. Who* is used when the person is the subject of the sentence: *Who* sneezed? *Whom* is used when the person is the object of a verb or a preposition: *Whom* can I thank?

An **object pronoun** may be used as the direct object or the indirect object of a verb or as the object of a preposition. The object pronouns are *me, you* (singular or plural), *him, her, it, us,* and *them:* I saw *her* at the mall. I showed *her* a great T-shirt. She bought it for *him.*

A **personal pronoun** has different forms.

- A personal pronoun shows **person:** the speaker **(first person),** the person spoken to **(second person),** or the person, place, or thing spoken about **(third person).** The first person pronouns are *I, me, mine, we, us,* and *ours.* The second person pronouns are *you* and *yours.* The third person pronouns are *he, him, his, she, her, hers, it, its, they, them,* and *theirs.*

- A personal pronoun shows **number: singular or plural.** A personal pronoun is **singular** when it refers to one person, place, or thing. A personal pronoun is **plural** when it refers to more than one person, place, or thing. The singular pronouns are *I, me, mine, you, yours, she, her, hers, he, him, his, it,* and *its.* The plural pronouns are *we, us, ours, you, yours, they, them,* and *theirs.*

- The third person singular personal pronoun can refer to a male (*he, him, his*), a female (*she, her, hers*), or a thing (*it, its*).

A **possessive pronoun** shows possession or ownership. The possessive pronouns are *mine, yours, his, hers, its, ours,* and *theirs.* Although possessive pronouns show ownership, they do not contain apostrophes: The new skates are *hers.*

A **reflexive pronoun** can be used as a direct object or an indirect object or as the object of a preposition. Reflexive pronouns usually refer to the subject of the sentence. The reflexive pronouns are *myself, yourself, himself, herself, itself, ourselves, yourselves,* and *themselves:* The man helped *himself.* He made *himself* a sandwich. Gwen walked by *herself.*

A **subject pronoun** may be used as the subject or as a subject complement. The subject pronouns are *I, you* (singular or plural), *he, she, it, we,* and *they.*

See also **antecedents.**

PUNCTUATION

An **apostrophe** (') is used as follows:

- to show ownership—the *cook's* hat, the *girls'* horses

- to replace a letter or letters left out in a contraction—*he'll* for *he will, I'm* for *I am*

Commas (,) are used to make reading clearer. Among the many uses of a comma are the following:

- to separate three or more words or groups of words in a series—We saw elephants, giraffes, hyenas, and monkeys.

- to set off parts of dates—January 1, 2009

- to set off parts of addresses—321 Spring Rd., Apt. 4

- to separate a city and a state—Atlanta, GA

- to set off words in direct address—Josie, I'm so pleased that you called me this morning.

- after the word *yes* or *no* when it introduces a sentence—Yes, I agree with you completely.

- to set off direct quotations, except where a question mark or an exclamation point is needed—
    "We have only vanilla and chocolate today," he said in an apologetic tone.
    "Fantastic!" Lena shouted.

- to separate independent clauses connected by the conjunctions *and, but,* and *or*—She called his name, but he didn't answer her.

- after the salutation in a friendly letter and the closing in all letters—Dear Ben, Sincerely yours,

An **exclamation point** (!) is used after an interjection or an exclamatory sentence: Wonderful! What a celebration that was!

A **period** (.) is used at the end of a declarative sentence or an imperative sentence and after initials and some abbreviations: Dr. H. L. Martin is here. Please invite him to sit down.

A **question mark** (?) is used at the end of a question: What time is it?

Quotation marks (" ") are used as follows:

- before and after every direct quotation and every part of a divided quotation—
    "Let's go shopping," said Michiko.
    "I can go with you," Father said, "after I have eaten lunch."

- to enclose titles of short stories, poems, songs, and magazine articles. Titles of magazines, newspapers, movies, plays, TV shows, works of art, and most books are usually printed in *italics* or are underlined—I read "A Tribute to Heroes" in *Time for Kids.*

SENTENCES

A **sentence** is a group of words that expresses a complete thought.

A **complex sentence** contains one independent clause and one dependent clause: After Frida caught a cold, she went to bed.

A **compound sentence** contains two or more independent clauses. An independent clause has a subject and a predicate, and it can stand alone as a sentence. A compound sentence is formed by connecting two independent clauses with a comma and the coordinating conjunction *and, but,* or *or.* A semicolon may be used instead of the comma and conjunction: We went to the park, *and* we played softball. It started to rain; we ran home.

A **declarative sentence** makes a statement. It ends with a period: The sun is shining.

An **exclamatory sentence** expresses strong or sudden emotion. It ends with an exclamation point: What a loud noise that was!

An **imperative sentence** gives a command or makes a request. It usually ends with a period: Go to the store. Please pick up the papers.

An **interrogative sentence** asks a question. It ends with a question mark: Where is my pen?

A sentence is made up of a subject and a predicate.

- The **subject** names the person, place, or thing a sentence is about. The **simple subject** is a noun or pronoun: The tall young *man* is riding. The **complete subject** is the simple subject with all the words that describe it: *The tall young man* is riding.

- The **predicate** tells something about the subject. The **simple predicate** is a verb or verb phrase: Teresa *waved* to the child. The **complete predicate** is the verb with all its objects, complements, and describing words: Teresa *waved to the child*.

- The **direct object** answers the question *whom* or *what* after an action verb in a sentence: Nathaniel fed the *baby*. An object pronoun can be used as a direct object: Nathaniel fed *him*.

- The **indirect object** tells to whom, for whom, to what, or for what an action is done. The indirect object comes between the verb and the direct object: Kim gave *Laura* a present.

- The **subject complement** is a word that completes the meaning of a linking verb in a sentence. A subject complement may be a noun, a pronoun, or an adjective: Broccoli is a green *vegetable*. The winner was *she*. The sea will be *cold*.

Sentence order is the sequence of the subject and verb in a sentence.

- When the verb in a sentence follows the subject, the sentence is in **natural order**: The *settlers planted* the seeds.

- When the main verb or the helping verb in a sentence comes before the subject, the sentence is in **inverted order**: Across the plain *marched* the tired *soldiers*.

If a sentence has two or more simple subjects, it has a **compound subject:** *Ivan* and *John* argued with the grocer.

If a sentence has two or more predicates, it has a **compound predicate:** The toddler *walks* and *plays* well.

If a sentence has two or more direct objects, it has a **compound direct object:** Wear your *hat, scarf,* and *gloves*.

If a sentence has two or more subject complements, it has a **compound subject complement:** The winners were *Steve* and *Patty*.

SUBJECT–VERB AGREEMENT

A subject and a verb must agree.

- Singular nouns, including noncount nouns, and third person singular pronouns (*he, she,* and *it*) take verbs that end in *-s* or *-es* in the simple present tense: Kendra *makes* maps. Laughter *makes* a nice sound.

- Plural nouns, plural pronouns, and the singular pronouns *I* and *you* must have verbs that do not end in *-s* or *-es*: We *run*. Cattle *run*.

- Use *am* or *was* with the first person singular pronoun: I *am* a soccer player. I *was* late for practice.

- Use *is* or *was* with a singular noun or a third person singular pronoun: Paris *is* a city. Fruit *is* nutritious. She *was* a pianist.

- Use *are* or *were* with a plural noun, the second person subject pronoun, or the third person plural pronoun: Dogs *are* good pets. You *are* the winner. We *were* happy. They *were* my neighbors.

- Use *doesn't* with a singular noun or a singular third person pronoun: He *doesn't* have a pencil. The furniture *doesn't* cost much. She *doesn't* have a pen.

- Use *don't* with a plural noun, a first person pronoun, a second person pronoun, or a third person plural pronoun: Buses *don't* stop here. We *don't* have to go. You *don't* have the tickets.

TENSE

The tense of a verb shows the time of its action.

- The **simple present tense** tells about something that is always true or about an action that happens again and again. I *play* the piano every afternoon.

- The **simple past tense** tells about an action that happened in the past. The past tense of regular verbs ends in *-ed*: Lucia *raced* to the end of the block.

- The **future tense** tells about an action that will happen in the future. The future tense can be formed with *will* and the present part of the verb: They *will come* to the game on Sunday. The future tense can also be made from a form of the verb *be* with *going to* and the present part of the verb: I *am going to play* shortstop.

- The **present progressive tense** tells what is happening now. The present progressive tense is formed with a present form of *be* and the present participle: He *is eating* his lunch now.

- The **past progressive tense** tells what was happening in the past. The past progressive tense is formed with a past form of *be* and the present participle: We *were snoring* loudly last night.

- The **future progressive tense** tells what will be happening in the future; the future progressive is formed with *will, be, am going to be, is going to be,* or *are going to be* and the present participle: They *are going to be celebrating* their birthdays next week. He *will be going* South.

- The **present perfect tense** tells about an action that happened at some indefinite time in the past or an action that started in the past and continues into the present time. The present perfect tense is formed with *has* or *have* and the past participle: We *have lived* here for two years.

- The **past perfect tense** tells about a past action that was completed before another action in the past. The past perfect tense is formed with *had* and the past participle: She *had finished* her homework by 6 o'clock.

- The **future perfect tense** tells about a future event that will be started and completed before another future event. The future perfect tense is formed with *will have* and the past participle: We *will have eaten* lunch by the time you get here.

VERBS

A **verb** is a word that expresses action or being.

A **linking verb** links a subject with a subject complement (a noun, a pronoun, or an adjective). Verbs of being are linking verbs: She *is* a teacher. The winner *was* he. The children *will be* happy.

A verb has four **principal parts:** the **present**, the **present participle**, the **past**, and the **past participle.**

- The present participle is formed by adding *-ing* to the present: jumping, singing. For verbs that end in *e*, drop the final *e* and add *-ing:* drive, driving. For verbs that end in a consonant following a vowel, double the consonant before adding *-ing:* stop, stopping. The present participle is often used with a form of the helping verb *be* (*am, is, are, was, were* or *been*).

- The past and the past participle of regular verbs are formed by adding *-d* or *-ed* to the present: bake, baked, jump, jumped. For verbs that end in a consonant following a vowel, form the past participle by doubling the consonant before adding *-ing:* hum, hummed. The past participle is often used with the helping verb *have, has,* or *had.*

- The simple past and the past participle of irregular verbs are not formed by adding *-ed* to the present: sang, sung.

A **verb phrase** is a group of words that does the work of a single verb. A verb phrase contains one or more helping verbs (such as *is, are, has, have, will, can, could, would, should*) and a main verb: She *had tripped* over the rug twice before I saw her.